What Others Are Saying About
Where There Was No Church

Gone are the days when the only people writing about Islam and its adherents were academics. Books by reflecting practitioners, such as this one, are complementing the scholars. Gone are the days when approaches to Muslims were sincere but mono-cultural. Books such as this one, take the cross-cultural task seriously by rolling up their sleeves and entering into the world of Muslim people, taking the gospel with them as a lifestyle. The contributors to this book work hard to reflect well on good practice and what resonates best with Muslim people as they follow Jesus Christ. It is therefore an invaluable read that already sits high on my most recommended reading list.

Steve Bell, author and trainer in Islam and Christian witness, England

This compilation of true stories is a must read for all who want to learn from the experiences of others. It gives great insights into the practices God is blessing in raising up Jesus followers among Muslims. With resources that have been developed over many years by a multi-agency team, this book will help to equip you for the task. Don't leave home without it!

Dr. J. Dudley Woodberry, Dean Emeritus and Senior Professor of Islamic Studies, School of Intercultural Studies, **Fuller Theological Seminary**, USA

With its compelling narratives illustrating solid research, this book doesn't attempt to give you all the answers, but it could well help you ask the right questions.

Dr. David Greenlee, PhD, International Research Associate, **OM**, Switzerland

Where There Was No Church helps us to understand new movements of people who may want to follow Christ if they understood Jesus and the Gospel in a new way. I commend these fantastic stories to you; they come from people who are not just theorists but also practitioners. May this book equip us to share Christ meaningfully in the modern world.

Dr. K. Rajendran, General Secretary, **India Missions Association** and Chairman, **World Evangelical Alliance Mission Commission**, India

Across the Muslim world, the Holy Spirit is quietly but powerfully writing a story of people coming to love and follow Jesus. This book tells something of that story. It calls us to pray believingly, to reach out in love and to witness wisely. Let's dare to join in the Spirit's story!

Mrs. Rose Dowsett, Vice-Chair, **World Evangelical Alliance Mission Commission**, Scotland

I have used *Where There Was No Church* in a small group setting to encourage creative ways to think about mission. Each person, no matter what their background or previous experience with cross-cultural ministry, could identify in some way with the stories. The book caused each of us to stop, think and pray for those who do not have the same freedoms as we do, and encouraged us to reexamine how we see and do church in our own context.

Rev. Lanny Arensen, International Director, **AIM**, England

This book brings together great stories of God at work in the Muslim world. As you read it, you will grow in expectancy, learning more of how to partner in what God is doing. I am certain that *Where There Was No Church* will help us to find a path to fruitful ministry among Muslims.

Mark Kim, International Director, **Global Operation**, Korea

Everyone who seeks to glorify God wants to bear fruit, but many faithfully serve and see little fruit. *Where There Was No Church* is a training manual that brings together stories of fruitfulness from those serving in some pretty tough places. I use *Where There Was No Church* with IMB workers as they prepare for ministry among unreached people groups.

Dr. Jim Haney, Director, Global Research **IMB**, USA

Church has historically been done in a doctrinal and political way, leading to denominations. But when it comes from stories like these, of the gospel moving in new areas like Islam, church is dynamic, reflecting the words of its founder: "I will build my church, and the gates of hell will not prevail against it."

David Bok, Bible teacher and cross-cultural facilitator who relates to Muslims through inter-religious dialogue, Southeast Asia.

Do you want to understand what principles are bearing fruit in pioneer church planting among Muslims? *Where There Was No Church* is a very helpful tool for Great Commission Christians who want to discover how we can be "workers together with God." You will learn how to analyse a ministry and better think through principles. You will also rejoice as you read about places where there are now Muslims who are "obedient to the faith." Highly recommended to those who love God with their minds as well as their hearts.

Dr. Greg Livingstone, Founder, **Frontiers**, England

Where There Was No Church

POSTCARDS FROM FOLLOWERS OF JESUS
IN THE MUSLIM WORLD

EJ MARTIN, EDITOR

Where There Was No Church:
Postcards from Followers of Jesus in The Muslim World
© 2010, 2020 by Vision 5:9

All rights reserved.

No part of this book may be reproduced, stored in a retrieval system, or transmitted in any form orby any means—electronic, mechanical, photocopy, recording, or otherwise—without prior writtenpermission of the publisher, except brief quotations used in connection with reviews in magazinesor newspapers. For permission, email permissions@wclbooks.com. For corrections, email editor@wclbooks.com.

Scriptures taken from the Holy Bible, New International Version®, NIV®. Copyright © 1973, 1978, 1984, 2011 by Biblica, Inc.™ Used by permission of Zondervan. All rights reserved worldwide. www.zondervan.com The "NIV" and "New International Version" are trademarks registered in the United States Patent and Trademark Office by Biblica, Inc.™

Cover design: David McNeill
Cover photo credit: Matt Brandon, www.thedigitaltrekker.com

Published by William Carey Publishing
10 W. Dry Creek Cir
Littleton, CO 80120 | www.missionbooks.org

William Carey Publishing is a ministry of Frontier Ventures
Pasadena, CA 91104 | www.frontierventures.org

ISBNs: 978-1-64508-327-6 (paperback), 978-1-64508-329-0 (mobi), 978-1-64508-330-6 (epub)

Printed Worldwide

24 23 22 21 20   2 3 4 5 6 IN

Library of Congress Control Number: 2020943138

Contents

Acknowledgements................................. ix
Preface..x

The Stories — 1

Not a Foreign Message 3
Couscous on Sunday................................15
Meeting the Saviour through the Quran 31
Desperate Enough to Pray 49
The Messiah Is Not a Liar...........................69
Stoking the Home Fire 85
Uncle, Is It True? 97

About the Stories — 111

What are Fruitful Practice Stories?....................113
Who has Conducted this Study?.....................113

Using the Stories — 115

Discussion Guides 117
   How to Use the Discussion Guides 117
   Discussion: Not a Foreign Message 118
   Discussion: Couscous on Sunday....................122
   Discussion: Meeting the Saviour through the Quran ..126
   Discussion: Desperate Enough to Pray...............129
   Discussion: The Messiah Is Not a Liar................132
   Discussion: Stoking the Home Fire..................135

    Discussion: Uncle, Is It True?......................139
Fruitful Practices.....................................143
    Introduction..143
    Categorization......................................148
    Relating to Society 149
    Relating to Seekers................................154
    Relating to Believers..............................159
    Relating to Leaders................................170
    Relating to God....................................174
    Communication Methods.........................177
    Fruitful Teams......................................184
    Characteristics of Fruitful Faith Communities 191
    Works Cited..201

Acknowledgements

Just a few years ago, I heard few stories of Muslims putting faith in Jesus. Many of those faced extreme circumstances of persecution. In their ones and twos, these brave souls were willing to give up everything in favour of the pearl of great price that is the kingdom of God. Today, there are certainly places where God's people are still faithfully sowing the seeds of the gospel and seeing very little fruit. In many places, still only the courageous ones and twos follow Christ on their own. Today we are seeing some situations in which communities of people are following Jesus together. Where it's not just ones and twos, but families of Muslims, or even networks of families, who have begun to follow Christ together. Acknowledging those who have paid the great price of persecution, I am grateful to those who have welcomed the messengers of Christ and whose stories are told here.

Eric Adams, Tom Benedict, CJ Daniels, Clare Janzen, and Andrea Gray have given their talents without charge to this project as reporter/authors. The organizations they serve have released their time so they could make their contributions. Fruitful Practice Research team members have provided the foundation of research on which this project was built. Special thanks also to Eric Adams, who nurtured the seed of the idea; Leon Torkko, for saying it was time to "get off the dime;" Angela Murray, for helping us believe it could go further; and John Becker, for stepping into the gap as a champion for the team.

Preface

The air was as still and sticky as ever that Monday night as we rode home. As we rounded the bend with the huge magnolia trees, their heady scent wafted through the window to me. My 8-year-old mind was still trying to figure out why Mama hadn't wanted me to go down to the front of the church. The preacher had invited us all, and lots of other people were streaming down to the altar. It made perfectly logical sense to me, what the man had said. Brother Eddie had quoted John 3:16 enough times that night that I had been able to memorize it. "For God so loved the world that he gave his only begotten son, that whosoever believeth in him should not perish, but have eternal life." I can still quote it today in the King James Version that Brother Eddie Martin, revival preacher, used that night.

Mama had wanted me to be sure I knew what I was doing. Today, I probably would say she was asking me to "count the cost." But that night, all I knew was that my heart had been bursting to say "yes" to Jesus.

At the end of the evening, Brother Eddie had invited us all to sing "Just As I Am," and if we wanted to accept Jesus as our personal Lord and saviour, well, we should come on down to that altar at the front of the First Baptist Church and get our lives right with God. So, on the 8th of May, 1969, I understood that I was a sinner in need of God's forgiveness through Jesus. And, in spite of Mama's reservations, I rushed down to the altar and asked him for it.

And he forgave me. And it was real.

That's how my story began. But the process of coming to faith in Christ can look very different in other cultures. This book tells stories that were very different from mine. In these stories, there were no community initiatives to "pack a pew" by inviting friends to come along to the revival meeting, no eager church members waiting at an altar to pray with repentant ones, in fact no altar at all. For them, there was no church.

These stories tell how people born as Muslims in predominantly Islamic countries began to follow Jesus Christ as Lord. They live in societies where, until recently, there was no active witness to the gospel.

Just like me, the followers of Jesus in these pages don't have everything worked out perfectly yet. But in their various ways, they have also encountered and accepted the same mercy and forgiveness offered by Jesus.

The stories that comprise the first half of this book also provide glimpses of the people from other cultures who entered their lives and introduced them to Jesus. What did these cross-cultural bearers of the gospel do to effectively present Jesus and help new believers follow him together?

What they did that bore fruit (something we call "fruitful practices") is the focus of the second half of the book. If you live among Muslims and invite them to follow Jesus with you, the second part of this book provides you with information and tools to help you reflect on that great work of the gospel.

Across the Muslim world, God is drawing new brothers and sisters into the body of Christ. And he is calling others to partner with him in that great work of his Spirit. It is my hope that the resources and stories in this book will inspire and equip you to take the good news of Jesus to the Muslim world.

EJ Martin

The Stories

The following stories are true stories about real people who are following Jesus the Messiah as Lord. To protect the privacy and security of those involved, the names have been changed and the location left unspecified. Minor details may have been changed in order to make the stories read smoothly as a story.

In the Islamic cultures where these stories are set, Jesus the Messiah is usually known by his Arabic name, Isa al Masih, and his good news is called the Injil.

Nabil reclined on a mattress on the floor with his mother and his six-year-old nephew, Ahmed. Nabil was trying to make funny faces to lighten their mood, to counteract the gloom that spilled over them as bomb blasts filled their ears. Nabil's sister, Sarah, came in with a sandwich and a cup of milk for her son, Ahmed. She had mixed up the milk powder with more water than usual. Who knew when they'd be able to get to the supermarket again? Or whether there would be any milk on the shelves when they did. Ahmed didn't seem to mind. He gulped down the milk in spite of its watery taste.

"Allah!" Sarah exclaimed as a nearby explosion rocked the building.

Although many families were trying to escape the bombing by fleeing to another town, most of Nabil's neighbours had nowhere to go. Even if they did, they couldn't afford to leave. It was rumoured that taxi drivers, the only ones who really knew the roads well enough to navigate the hazardous route quickly, were charging ten times the normal fare to drive people out of the city. That would be almost a month's salary for Nabil.

Sarah felt overwhelmed. She flopped down on the cushions and began to weep loudly. "Pull yourself together! Be strong for the sake of the child!" her mother told her.

Sarah sighed and sat up against some cushions, burying her head in her hands. Earlier that day, Nabil and Sarah had pulled all their mattresses and blankets into the tiny hallway that led to all the rooms in the flat. By shutting all the doors, they made a little room that had no windows, except for the opening that led to the kitchen, but they had covered the kitchen window with tape to protect themselves from flying glass. It was safer, they hoped, but it was also darker, and the electricity had been off for a while.

Ahmed finished his sandwich and milk and reached for Nabil's mobile phone. The light that came on when Ahmed began to push buttons randomly gave Nabil an idea. He opened the door to the guest room and brought back a wooden stand with a Bible on it. He took Ahmed into his lap and showed him how to point the phone towards the words on the page. Nabil turned to the section called the Psalms of David and located Psalm 23, one of his favourites. The imagery of shepherds and sheep evoked images of the fields outside his grandparents' village. Though he'd never been to their village, he felt he knew it as well as the town where his parents had come as exiles and where he had been born.

"The Lord is my shepherd," Nabil began in Arabic.

Sarah looked up. "What is this?" she interrupted.

Nabil drew himself up. "These are the Psalms of the Prophet David, peace be upon him." His sister propped herself up against some cushions and listened. She closed her eyes and let her mind wander to her grandparents' village, to the ancient family home and the fertile orchards. If only we could return to that paradise now, she thought. But in her heart, she knew it no longer existed. Perhaps all the houses had been destroyed by those who had driven her grandparents and the other villagers out, or maybe settlers now occupied the ancient houses. Either way, if she ever got a chance to go back there, it would not match up with the stories her grandparents had told. For a moment, her fear turned to hatred toward those who had driven her grandparents from their home and were now trying to destroy her own generation. "God, where are you? Why don't you destroy our enemies?" she wondered.

Nabil turned to another Psalm and continued reading:

> Though a thousand fall at your side,
> Though ten thousand are dying around you,
> These evils will not touch you.

More explosions sounded nearby. "I take refuge in God," their mother mumbled, fingering her prayer beads.

> If you make the Lord your refuge,
> If you make the Most High your shelter,
> No evil will conquer you;
> No plague will come near your dwelling.

Sarah continued to listen as her brother read from the Psalms of the Prophet David. She was strangely comforted by the ancient words. For almost an hour, Nabil read Psalm after Psalm. Now it was dark outside, and Ahmed was asleep.

His grandmother laid him gently on a mattress and covered him with a thick blanket. Even though it was the middle of summer and the weather was hot and sticky, she didn't want to put her grandson at risk to catch a cold by sleeping uncovered. Sarah laid herself down next to her son and tried to rest.

Nabil slipped quietly into the kitchen and filled a glass of water from the tap. His voice was hoarse from reading, but he was thankful that God had shown him a way to comfort his sister. And he thanked God that he had let himself be convinced to start reading the Bible in Arabic instead of English. What if there had been only an English Bible in their home? How much would his sister have understood? Even if she had understood the words, would the Psalms in English have comforted her? And what about his mother? She wouldn't have understood any of it.

Nabil thought back a few years to the time when he first started talking to Pete and Dave, the Americans he worked with, about God and the prophets and about their respective holy books. He enjoyed getting together with them. Although they were fun-loving and ready to joke, they also seemed respectable and God-fearing. They didn't fit his previous image of Westerners. So it wasn't long before he started asking them questions about their spiritual practices, such as prayer and fasting. He also had some questions about the Bible. Because they worked in English and his fluency in English far exceeded theirs in Arabic, these early conversations had been in English. Soon, however, Pete and Dave began to improve in Arabic to the point that most of their conversations shifted into Nabil's language.

Not a Foreign Message | 7

One day, Pete and Dave introduced Nabil to their friend Terry. He wasn't in the country for a long visit, but he and Nabil hit it off, so they spent a lot of time together. They visited each other and had long conversations about Jesus over thick Turkish coffee and then read the Bible together. Since Terry spoke no Arabic, they always read from the English Bible and spoke English together. Nabil loved Jesus and he loved reading about Jesus and the apostles in the Bible. Eventually his love for Jesus grew into a desire to serve him, and Nabil began to count himself as one of the followers of Jesus.

Nabil was well-respected in his work place, and many of his friends and co-workers were eager to hear what he had to say about his encounter with Jesus. After about a year, one of his close friends, Sami, also decided to become a follower of Jesus. Together, Nabil and Sami would invite their friends to

Photo credit:Matt Brandon, www.thedigitaltrekker.com

meet together on their day off to read the Bible and discuss what they read.

Nabil thought back to one of those early meetings. A group of young men was lounging on low couches around the guest room in Sami's family home. Sami's wife had made them coffee and then had left them alone to study and talk. He remembered how he had taken his treasured copy of the Bible out of his brief case. He had opened up the Bible and read a passage from the Good News of Matthew: "Don't store up treasures here on earth where they can be eaten by moths ... ."

Then the group launched into a discussion of the passage in Arabic. Their discussion had been fruitful. At least his friends were thinking about the teachings of Jesus and asking questions.

Later, Nabil told Pete and Dave about the success of the meeting. They were really encouraged, but then as he pulled out his Bible to show them a verse the group had discussed, they realized that Nabil had been reading the Bible only in English. "Why English?" they asked. "Is there anyone in the group who doesn't speak Arabic?" Nabil told them he felt it was more prestigious to read in English, and that was the language in which he himself had first encountered the Bible.

Then Dave challenged him, "Don't you think it would connect with people's hearts more strongly if you read the Bible in Arabic?"

Nabil was open to the idea of holding their meetings only in Arabic. The next time the group met, as they finished their coffee, he glanced up at the Quranic verse framed on the wall opposite him. "God is the light of the heavens and the earth," it read in beautiful Arabic calligraphy. Nabil was suddenly confident that God could reveal his message in Arabic as well as in English. He prayed for God to guide them as they listened to God's revelation – this time in Arabic.

For the first time since the group had begun meeting together, Nabil picked up the Arabic Bible from the table in front of him, opened it, and read the passage to be studied in Arabic. To his surprise, he found that more of the young men were participating and that they seemed to grasp the message better. He even noticed that they seemed to be interacting with the issues they discussed from their heart, rather than just their minds. "What do you think about only reading the Bible in Arabic?" he asked the others after they had finished the main part of their discussion.

One member of the group spoke up. "When you read in English, it was confusing for us. Sometimes we didn't understand what the passage meant."

Another said, "We didn't understand why the Bible had to be read in English. We didn't know why English was better than Arabic." Nabil then realized that communicating with his friends in the language of their heart was essential to helping them grow in faith.

The sound of an explosion nearby brought Nabil back to the present. He finished his glass of water and went back into the hallway where he found his family asleep. Let them sleep, he thought. Nights are the worst for bombing, and they will be awake soon enough. He carried the Arabic Bible and its stand back to the guest room. He was glad that Pete and Dave had encouraged him to read the Bible in Arabic with his friends.

The whole family slept late into the next day, having been awakened several times in the night by bombing. They were out of coffee anyway, so it was just as well that they slept through the early morning coffee time that Nabil loved to share with his sister. With the music of the famous singer Fairouz playing on the radio, and the rest of the family just waking up, their morning coffee time usually gave Nabil and Sarah the chance to confide in each other. On this particular morning, Sarah put together a breakfast with odds and ends. She hadn't been out to buy vegetables in a few days and what she did have was starting to wither in the summer heat. Perhaps if Nabil went out today …

After breakfast, Nabil decided to go by his work place to see if anyone was going to be at work that day. He called out at the gate and exchanged greetings with the old guard who came shuffling out of his shelter. It seemed no one had been there since the bombing started. "God help us!" the guard exclaimed and went back into his shelter. Nabil left and went to the apartment of his friend, Sami.

Sami greeted him with kisses on both cheeks and led him into the guest room where his wife served them coffee. Since Nabil was a close family friend, she remained in the room, exchanging news and asking about Nabil's mother and sister. "Sarah was really shaken up by the bombing last evening," Nabil confided. Nabil turned to Sami and said, "I read to Sarah from the Psalms of David. It was really comforting for her, and for Mama too. Do you remember how we used to read the Bible in English at our discussion times?" Sami nodded and laughed. Nabil went on, "I'm really glad that we started reading the Bible in Arabic with our friends. That experience made me realise that the message of God needs to be in the language of their heart. And that's especially true with our families."

Sami's wife excused herself and went back to her household tasks. As she left the room, Sami motioned in his wife's direction. "I've begun to read to her from the Injil every night," he whispered. Nabil looked up on a high shelf at the Arabic New Testament that Sami had placed on an ornate stand. A lamp was positioned above the stand and Nabil knew that, had there been electricity, the light would have been shining on the holy book.

Nabil responded to his friend, "It's good for her to hear the words of the Injil at the same time as she sees the signs of it in your life." Nabil paused and thought of his own faith journey. Then he continued, "My family has definitely seen the difference in my life that has come from following our Lord Jesus. I was never very religious as a youth. In fact, I'm not really religious now in terms of outward practices and habits – although of course I still pray and fast – but they can see that I am serious about obeying God. My mother even said that I seem more like her son now than before I believed in our Lord Jesus."

"It's true," Sami confirmed, "they can see the spark in your life." Then he went on, "do you remember when you first began following our Lord Jesus, and you were really outspoken in telling people about him at work? For me, I'm like that with my own family, but for those in my clan, I'm taking it more slowly."

"Is that because your clan is a bit more traditional? That you still make decisions as a group?"

Sami nodded. "I am just doing subtle things, like putting that Injil up there. And I am sowing seeds here and there, sharing about our Lord Jesus little by little until there are enough people to decide by consensus to follow him. And most of them don't know English. I could never reach them without using the Arabic Injil."

"By the way," Nabil asked, "does your family know English?" Nabil meant Sami's wife, but out of politeness, did not refer to her specifically.

"Not a word," Sami replied. "My wife is very smart, but she didn't finish her education. And my children also do not know English. Not yet, anyway – oh!" Sami interrupted himself. "Let me show you something." He went out of the room and came back with a box of cassettes. "These are the stories of the prophets, peace be upon them. They aren't in our dialect, but we can understand them. I love that they use our traditional music too. When I first heard these stories, I said, 'This is our language. This is our message. This is not a foreign message.' I listen to them in the car as I travel for my job, and I feel so close to God when I listen to them. Eventually I will let my family listen to them."

Nabil's eyes lit up, "I would love to listen to those stories. I really like some of the cassettes I got from Dave that have some inspirational prayers and messages about the Injil, but I think stories of the prophets would be useful for my family."

Sami and Nabil enjoyed a long discussion. Finally Nabil got up to leave. "I promised my mother and sister I'd try to find some vegetables," he said.

As Nabil was leaving, Sami's wife handed him a black plastic bag with a bunch of locally-grown bananas in it. "These are for little Ahmed," she said.

"God bless your hands," he said. After a prolonged leave-taking, he continued on his way through the neighbourhood. He bought some tomatoes, cucumbers and potatoes for an exorbitant price and then ducked into a supermarket run by a family friend. As predicted, there was no more powdered milk, but Nabil bought some cans of tuna and sardines and some processed cheese before heading to the bakery to pick up some fresh bread. Even war didn't shut down the local bakeries. They were part of the foundation of the neighbourhood.

Sarah received the supplies gratefully. Nabil knew that his mother and sister were creative enough to come up with a wonderful meal no matter what he brought home to them. Later that evening, as they sat down to a pleasant meal of salad, fried potatoes and sardines, Nabil picked up a loaf of pita bread and the plate of sardines. "Did you know," he said to Ahmed, "that our master Jesus once performed a miracle with just a few loaves of bread and a few fishes?"

Ahmed shook his head and said between bites of banana, "Tell me the story, uncle!"

Epilogue

The violence in Nabil and Sami's area eventually ended, and normal life resumed for their families. Due to the violence, the group of young men who used to meet to discuss the Bible dispersed. Sami and Nabil turned their attention to their family and clan networks. Nabil's sister, Sarah, and their mother have since become enthusiastic followers of Jesus, as have Sami's wife and daughter.

Andrea Gray *has worked for ten years in Asia and Africa. She is involved in research, consulting and collaborative outreach projects with Muslims and Christians.*

Couscous on Sunday

by Souad Imani & Tom Benedict

When you're a child, your own life defines normal. Your house is painted white outside, and comfortable. Other houses in the neighbourhood are white, too, and are also probably furnished with couches covered in richly coloured fabric with golden trim. Every ceiling in the neighbourhood is decorated with intricate plaster carvings with a chandelier suspended from the centre of the design. The walls around each property all keep out the same thieves. And so you assume that mothers and fathers inside all those other houses love each other, that other fathers are gone for most of the week, and that brothers and sisters are all treated equally, with older brothers being responsible to protect their sisters. And once a week they all eat mountains of steamed semolina draped with savoury orange pumpkin and carrots and cabbage and turnips and chickpeas and more, and if they're lucky, lamb or beef or chicken buried down in the middle. Couscous.

Certainly all of our neighbours enjoy couscous the way we do. Yet over time, I notice that my family are somehow different. This dawns on me via small revelations at first. Imagine my little-girl-shock when I discover that other families eat their couscous on Fridays! We've been eating couscous on Sundays for as long as I can remember, though my father and mother say it wasn't always so for them. I notice this about the time I start to go to school, and so I begin to watch, to notice. And to wonder.

I learn that there are reasons we eat couscous on Sundays. My father works and sleeps at different times than the rest of us, and he isn't always awake when we are. We rarely see him during the week, but on Sundays he makes up for it, filling the day with his presence. This alone makes Sundays special, and couscous is what you eat on the special day during the week. I suspect that for us children it may also happen the other way around; couscous makes the day special. (Adults probably think this way, too, but they never admit to things like this.) Either way, on Sundays my father helps us to see that we are different, and how that is a good thing. All of us believe him. But there are other special days I don't understand so well, such as the Id al Adha, the Great Feast.

Others celebrate it, we don't. So I grow up seeing it from across the street, not completely sure what it's about. Our neighbours prepare for the feast over many weeks, saving up so they can buy a sheep for the family. The men go to a sheep market and choose their victim; they bargain until sunset if necessary to make sure the vendor is tired and just wants to go home, so he will give a good price. And having bargained until all the tea is gone, the buyer bundles up the doomed creature, perhaps onto the back of a motorbike, and drives it home. But not my father.

I watch a few neighbours bring their sheep home, but there are dozens, even hundreds in the area, all of them bringing a sheep home to live on a roof terrace or balcony until the feast, which might still be weeks away, and they use these weeks to fatten up the sorry creatures a bit longer. For many days before the feast, I go to sleep and wake up to a thousand fearful bleatings, which drown out the roosters. All of this is normal – except that we don't have a sheep on our own terrace.

Then the day of the Great Feast comes. I look out our window in the morning and the streets are mostly quiet except for a few boys calling out, offering to sharpen knives for a good price. Men and boys are on the terraces because it's almost time to start cooking, and then I hear shouting or a terrified animal screaming for help, which shatters the peace. And little by little the bleating stops until there is a stillness that doesn't feel like a holiday at all, and then bloody water flows in the gutters while the stench of entrails blows through the house.

Still, being different during Id al Adha doesn't seem like a major thing because families tend to stay to themselves during holidays. But I keep looking out of the window, and when I go back to school after the holiday, I see new clothes peeking out from under other girls' school smocks. And I learn to wait for Christmas, because in our home that's when I may get some new clothes.

I see differences, and the neighbour kids do, too, sometimes mercilessly so, despising me because of those differences they see. Other students treat me badly at school. They become angry and call me and our whole family names, names I don't understand except I know they're bad names.

"You are Jews," they say. As a child I don't know much about Jews, but I know two things: we are Christians not Jews, and they hate Jews. I am hurt and confused.

My father tries to help us understand. He tells us that we don't need to sacrifice sheep anymore, because Jesus has become the Lamb of God for us, and we only need to believe in him. Later I understand this better, but at the time I am content with what my father teaches us, that following Jesus is not only the most important thing in life, it is the only thing in life. This is who we are.

So when I get back to school after Id al-Adha, everybody is noticing I don't have new clothes. I am different. Not just at school, either. People know the others who live in the neighbourhood. They know when neighbours are at home and when they have gone out. Some of the other fathers work at the same place as my father. So they think they all know me and my family and what it means that we're Christians, even though they get their ideas about Christians from the television because they think the only Christians in our country are foreigners. They think being a Christian means we eat pork, believe in three Gods and are dirty, immoral people. And my family doesn't do or teach those horrible things, but I don't know how to convince them.

I wish they could know my parents. Even though my father is strong, he is a humble man. He insists that we worship God every Sunday and study the Holy Book. And he always teaches us. But he doesn't think he is so strong. He says that he would never grow in his faith unless other people help him. At one time, some of the people who helped him to study the Holy Book were foreigners, but there were others like us, too.

Couscous on Sunday | 19

I have memories of when I was very young, cloudy memories. Our family is going to a church in the city centre, which is far from where we live. In the morning foreigners meet there, and in the afternoon we worship God and sing and pray with others in our own language, and I even study in a Holy Book class with some other children. We enjoy meeting there with others who are like us because they also are different from their neighbours. One family has a daughter who is about my age, and we try to be friends, but it doesn't work between us because she's a city girl and her parents can afford to buy her fancy clothes and she looks down her nose at country girls like me. And so we argue a lot when we see each other, which I later realise is stupid. It is also not normal for me, as I prefer to be quiet. But there are other children and mothers and fathers who are kind to us, and it feels like they are family. And so we continue to see them every week, and often we spend the day with them and eat a meal and laugh together.

Photo Credit: iStockPhoto.com

Then after a while, the police came and they stopped the church meeting. They found a list on the wall saying who would be doing what role in the worship next week. They took all those people to the police station for questioning, including my father. But this didn't upset him, because he wasn't afraid. The police had come to talk to him many times, and my mother told me that he had even been in prison before. When he was in prison, colleagues where he works, his Muslim friends who know him as a good man, were the ones who convinced the police to let him go.

This time, after he is released, we return to worshipping and studying the Holy Book with others on Sundays in our home.

My parents are always concerned that we are behaving ourselves. For example, they always know where I am and what I am doing, so they calculate how long it takes for me to walk to and from school. My mother watches the clock every day to make sure I arrive home on time without getting into some kind of trouble. Sometimes I need to run home because class finishes late, and I am afraid I will be in trouble. At first I think this is a rule my parents have only for me and my sister, so they can be seen by others as protecting their daughters. But later I discover that they do this with my brothers, too. People know this about us, and perhaps it helps them to respect us, but we cannot force this from them.

Somehow life doesn't seem as hard for my brothers because they are strong. They will stand up to boys who say rude things, which I cannot do. And also, they are able to play football in the street because this is what boys do, and perhaps boys think playing football is more important than being a Jew. It's true that life is hard for them, too, but I don't think it is hard for them like it is for me.

They are also brave in school. A teacher once taught my eldest brother's class about Id al-Adha, in order to prepare them for the celebration. She told them, "During the feast we slaughter a sheep because we are celebrating how the prophet Ibrahim was willing to sacrifice his son to Allah. But Allah stopped him and provided a sacrifice in the boy's place. However, it is not required that everyone sacrifice a sheep during Id al-Adha, but only if the family has enough money to buy one." After that lesson, the children went home for the holiday to celebrate the feast.

When they returned to school, she asked, "Please, let us know how your family celebrated. Everyone whose family sacrificed a sheep during the holiday, please raise your hand."

Everyone except my brother raised a hand. So the teacher asked him, "So, is it the case that your family doesn't have the money to buy a sheep?"

"No, teacher. It is not because of money that we don't buy a sheep, it is because we are Christians."

Immediately everyone in the class started talking or yelling or laughing and the teacher had a hard time controlling them and didn't know what to say. She turned red and became very angry. And she took my brother to the head teacher's office.

On that very same day, my younger brother's class was memorising the Quran. He decided not to do this anymore, so he used his hands to cover his ears. "What are you doing?" the teacher asked. "Please listen as we read from the Holy Quran."

He shook his head. "No. I don't want to listen to those words anymore."

"Why not?" she demanded.

"Because our family are Christians," he said. And she became angry and took him to the head teacher's office.

So on the same day, two teachers made reports about how my brothers were causing problems in the classroom, and the head teacher telephoned my father, asking him to come and talk.

My father came to the school dressed in a coat and tie. He was calm and explained that he was very sorry for any disturbance caused by his sons in the classroom. He said he would speak with them and make sure that the boys behave themselves. My father made it clear that he would not apologise to the head teacher for our family's beliefs.

The head teacher begins to like my father, and they become friends. Through the years, they visit in each other's homes and drink tea together and talk about the things of God, which my father loves to do. In every conversation, he will speak of the goodness and love of God. And he also likes to speak about the holiness of God.

My father believes that the holiness of God is one of the most important subjects to talk about. This is because without understanding God's holiness, someone cannot understand how much sinful people need a saviour. He's right, but that doesn't change the fact that nobody else wants to be friends with me, because they think being a Christian is like a sickness; they stay away because they think I have a disease.

Even the teachers are affected.

One time, when the teacher told the class to go out and play during their fifteen minutes of break time, I had to stay inside.

The other teachers said they wanted to understand me. They talked to me the way adults usually talk, and I trusted them the way children are supposed to trust adults. At first, they seemed to want to be friendly with me. They asked questions about my parents and my brothers and sisters. "Are they all Christians?" They wanted to know what religious things we did in our house. They even asked some other teacher friends to come over to talk to me.

"Will you show us how you pray?" they asked. "We want to know how Christians pray."

"Of course!" I answered. This seemed like a chance to help them to understand. And because they were smiling, they seemed nice. So I folded my hands and closed my eyes, and began to pray.

"Oh God, will you please bless my father at his work and my mother who does all the work at home, and our auntie who is ill now. And will you please bless my brothers and sister with all they have to do in school, and I make all these prayers in Jesus' name." But it was hard to finish the prayer because before I finished, I started hearing them laughing at me.

"How could anyone be so stupid?"

"Who do they think they are, bringing up their children this way?"

"Can you imagine that people actually believe that there are three Gods?"

And I don't understand why a teacher would laugh at me because I am a child and I am praying and praying is a good thing and teachers are supposed to be good so they should be happy with me since I am praying. But they are laughing instead because they think I am a bad person and a stupid person. And though this is hard for me, it gets even worse.

Most of the rest of the time they just ignore me. Day after day and week after week they act like I don't exist. They make me sit in the last seat in the classroom where nobody will see me. It doesn't matter whether I want to ask a question, or if I want to answer theirs. For long periods of time, for days on end, they don't speak to me. Not at all.

And it's pretty much the same with the other children. They don't want to be with me, or even speak to me. At least not in a friendly way.

"No, we can't play with you. You're sick!"

"Teacher says we're not allowed to talk with you."

And so I learn the difference between everyone else and my family: they think they are well and my family are ill and to be avoided.

This is pretty much what I remember about elementary school. Teachers ignore me or are mean to me. They give me failing marks for no reason. Other children ignore me, too. They won't play with me. I have no friends there.

For my brothers, things are only a little different. Sometimes they can't stand the way that people treat them, so they get angry and get into fights. And because they are fighting back, others leave them alone more.

One day when I was small, some policemen came to our home and my brothers were playing together outside. They went up to the policemen to greet them, putting out their hands to shake, but the policemen would not shake them. The policemen looked angry.

They entered our home while my mother was visiting with our neighbour and the police started yelling at her. They were getting more and more angry. My mother and the neighbour looked afraid, and they both started to cry.

"Where is your husband?" they screamed.

"He's at work now," my mother answered, lips quivering as she looked at our neighbour who was leaving through the back door because she doesn't want to get in trouble. Nobody stopped her.

"Where are his books?" they shouted, just centimetres from her face. "Where does he keep those books of lies?" My mother could only look at them silently. I had never seen her so afraid, and I never understood why they considered a Holy Book to be a book of lies.

Then one of them came up to my mother and said some things to her which I can't repeat because it was so awful. And then I was scared, too, and my mother held me in her arms and we sat there quietly for a long time. And when my father came home, they started yelling again and then they took him out the door and we didn't know when we would see him again and so my mother kept holding me and we prayed, because God is always listening and it was the only thing we knew how to do. And we didn't sleep much that night even though it was dark. The next day our prayers were answered and my father came home and that made us happy, even though we were still frightened at the same time. Then it was over, at least for the time being, and we all understood that we wouldn't talk about it.

When things like this are happening to my parents, it isn't right to burden them with my problems at school. The truth is, they have so many problems of their own that none of us can tell them what we're going through. I think they know, even though these are things we don't talk about. We all just know they're happening.

Not everyone treats us horribly, though. We have relatives in the countryside who are kind. I think it was difficult for my father and mother a long time ago, but eventually the family accept us, even if they disagree with us. One of my uncles always comes to stay with us when he has business in our city. In fact, there are always many people coming to stay in our home. This is a lot of work for my mother, and it is expensive for my parents, but they always welcome people to stay. And everybody knows that people go where they feel welcome.

Another uncle has had many problems in his family, and unfortunately he is divorced from his first wife. He has a teenage daughter who is hard for him to raise and his new wife doesn't want this daughter in the house, so they ask my parents if she may come and live with us. They ask because they know my parents will raise her correctly, but my parents are getting older and are praying for wisdom in this decision before they answer.

With time, our relatives and a few of our neighbours come to accept who we are. Some also believe in Jesus now! There are women who come to visit with my mother, and she visits them.

My father always leads our family in worshipping God on Sundays in our living room. Sometimes there are others with us for worship time; sometimes it is just our family.

Often those who come stay for a meal, because they come a long way to be with us. This is very regular; we always meet together sitting on our sofas and have a time of singing worship songs and reading the Holy Book on Sunday. He can't do this with us during the week because most of the time he needs to be at work all night, and so he is out while we sleep and he sleeps while we are awake. But he is always careful to teach us that we should read from the Holy Book every day for ourselves. He frowns at us and tells us this is our responsibility, and we can see his smile underneath his bushy moustache.

So my brother and I always get up early to read together before we go to school, about 5:30 in the morning. One of us reads the verses aloud, and the other reads some commentary or explanation on the verses. And then we pray together. We do this every day for maybe an hour. And this is how my faith is built up through the years.

There are things that even as a little girl I really like about my parents' life and their example to me. The main thing is how they treat each other. I never, ever hear my parents arguing with each other, or saying bad words to each other. They are always very careful not to do this in front of us. And so I know that my father respects my mother and my mother respects my father, which is a good thing, and it is not like other families I've seen. Many families I know have divorced parents. Or it is before the time of divorce and the husband is beating his wife.

When someone asks my father how he learned to be such a husband, he answers that he has been very blessed. He has the help of God in the present, and he also says that he had a good example in his own Muslim father, who was a very thoughtful and sensitive man.

And because when we were young my father was often away working, he also gives credit to my mother for raising us. He says that through her life, she is the best teacher he knows.

All of us are grown now, and the house is still very much like it was. There are photos of us spread around the living room, many from our weddings. And there are photos of grandchildren, because this very important for grandparents. Those of us who are married and have children are beginning to raise them to believe in Jesus also. In some ways, times are better because we are not so worried that the police will visit us. There are many more who are following Jesus Christ in my country than when I was young. Many people in my country now know that.

But we still must work hard to make sure that our children are reading the Bible and praying in our family and, when we can, we make sure to get together with others who believe. In our country, the numbers of those who believe in Jesus are growing, but so are the numbers of fundamentalists who would oppose us. We don't know what our children may have to suffer for following Christ, so they must be ready. They must come to know, as I have done, that God is always with us, that he keeps his promise, that his life is in us, and that is the only thing in the world which no one can take away from us.

My father now says that while it's true that Jesus died for our sins so that we could be forgiven and cleansed from sin, and that because of this we can go to heaven, this is not the reason Jesus did this for us. Rather, he says that the reason

Jesus died for us and rose again is so that we can become God's children and enjoy being part of God's family.

It's true. I have learned that God is always with his family no matter what other people do, and I pray that my children will know this, too.

Tom Benedict has lived cross-culturally for 25 years and feels privileged to be a friend of Souad and her family.

Meeting the Saviour through the Quran

by CJ Daniel

Just six weeks after he left his Western homeland to move to the Middle East, Abu Roo found himself in his living room opening the Quran and his Bible with four Muslim guests. These men, all students from an English class Abu Roo was teaching, had accepted his invitation to come to his home for a holy book study.

They came because Abu Roo had demonstrated a deep spirituality in his personal life, while at the same time rendering respect to their religion. From the very first day of class when Abu Roo stood up to address his students, he had made his spirituality clear to them. He faced questions such as "Who are you?" "Why are you here?" "What makes you different from the other Christians we know?" To these questions, Abu Roo answered honestly, using words that would communicate a correct understanding. Abu Roo says, "The last thing I wanted to do was to deceive anyone. I chose my words carefully saying, 'You need to understand that I am a man of God. That means I study the Word of God. I read all of the holy books – the Torah, the Psalms, Injil, and the Quran. I am also a man of prayer, a man of peace, and I am a follower of Isa al Masih.'"

From the beginning, Abu Roo invited his listeners to dialog with him. He would say, "I believe I may know some spiritual truths that you do not know, and I also believe you may have insight on things that I may not know. Why don't we, who are serious about our relationship with God, share our insights together as friends?"

Every day, as a teacher, Abu Roo lived out his spiritual life openly in front of his class. He would talk about answered prayer and would relate insights he was learning from God. He would talk about the nature and character of God. As he did so, he would refer to both the Quran and the Bible.

Abu Roo had been allowed to design the curriculum for an advanced English conversation course. He chose leadership as the topic of conversation. When the students began their discussion, they defined leadership and came to the conclusion that there are good and bad leaders. Then Abu Roo asked his students, "who do you think have been the greatest leaders in the history of the world?" As he expected, Muhammad and Jesus topped their lists. He then led them in a discussion about why they picked these two men.

"They were amazed that I knew as much as I did about the life of the Prophet," Abu Roo recalls, "and they were very attentive when I told them about the life of Jesus which had been veiled to them by their traditions."

During one class, Abu Roo opened his Bible to the story of Jesus and the expert in the Law. He read Matthew 22:36-40: "'Teacher, which is the greatest commandment in the Law?'

Jesus replied: 'Love the Lord your God with all your heart and with all your soul and with all your mind. This is the first and greatest commandment. And the second is like it: 'Love your neighbour as yourself. All the Law and the Prophets hang on these two commandments.'"

Abu Roo asked his class, "What do you think the world would be like if we were all faithful and obedient to this precept?"

In other class periods, Abu Roo brought up the subject of servant leadership. When he dealt with this and other leadership topics, he continually referred both to the Quran and the Bible.

His behaviour raised questions in the minds of his students. Abu Roo comes from a country his students consider a "Christian nation." Many of his students assume people from "Christian" countries smoke, drink, sleep around and believe abominable things. They think Christians worship three gods and believe God came down to have sex with Mary to produce Jesus. But to them, Abu Roo evidently lived the life of a genuine spiritual man. "They couldn't figure that out, with me not being a Muslim," Abu Roo says.

One day after class, a student came up to Abu Roo and began asking him spiritual questions and challenged the truth of the Bible. Abu Roo asked, "Would you like to come to my home where we could study the holy books together?"

The student replied, "I'd like to do that."

A young man standing behind him overheard the conversation and asked, "Can I come too?"

Another nearby student chimed in, "I'd also like to come."

And then another!

"Next thing I know," recalls Abu Roo, "I have four hard core Muslim guests in my home."

Abu Roo's first takers couldn't have been a more intimidating group. One, sporting a thick, full beard and dressed like a cleric, lectured in Islamic studies at a nearby university. Another followed the deeply conservative Wahhabi branch of Islam. The remaining two visitors hailed from the hometown of a famous Muslim terrorist and openly expressed sympathy for militant Islam. One of them, at the age of 12, had completely memorized the Quran from cover-to-cover and had recited it on television, receiving a national award for his accomplishment.

How could Abu Roo possibly share his faith with these men who were so steeped in Islamic tradition and so well-learned

Photo credit: Matt Brandon, www.thedigitaltrekker.com

from the Quran? Abu Roo had told them he wanted to discuss with them several signs from Allah that he had discovered in the Quran, and he wanted to know their thoughts about these signs.

The study Abu Roo uses originates from the importance placed on signs in the Quran itself. "The Quran indicates that a true unbeliever is one who denies or rejects the signs of Allah," Abu Roo explains, referring to Surah 7:36. "So the question then becomes, 'What are these signs?'" Abu Roo has found that most of his Muslim friends do not know what the signs of Allah are. "Yet," he says, "the Quran, as well as Scripture, is replete with signs, or miracles with spiritual truths attached, from God."

The Seven Signs study tracks a theme within these signs. From the beginning of creation, it traces God's grace, mercy, and His plan to provide salvation to mankind. Each of the seven studies focuses on a historic figure and their stories from the Bible and Quran: Adam, Noah, Abraham, Moses, David, Jonah, and finally Jesus. The first two studies focus on what God has done for us; the second two deal with how he accomplished this; then the last three deal with through whom he has done this.

The first sign comes from the story of creation as found in Genesis and the Quran. The Quran says that after Adam and Eve disobeyed God, clothing was provided by God to cover their nakedness, but it goes on to say that God also provided a "garment of righteousness" which is described as "the best gift" and "a sign" (Surah 7:26).

Abu Roo's four guests each held their own copy of the Quran and looked at him expectantly. He plunged right in. He began the study by reading from his Yusuf Ali English translation of the Quran. To start the conversation, he turned to the verse that says Allah made Adam "vice-regent" over the world: "Behold, thy Lord said to the angels: 'I will create a vice-regent on earth'" (2:30).

Abu Roo said, "This word, 'vice-regent,' is an old word, and we don't really use it much anymore in English. What does it mean in Arabic?"

One of the men said, "It is the word 'khalifah.'"

Abu replied, "Okay, so what does 'khalifah' mean?"

The men turned to each other discussing back and forth in the local language. Their spokesperson was the university lecturer who said, "Mr. Abu Roo, we do not know. We must call."

He picked up his cell phone, dialled a number, then began to converse with someone on the other end. Abu Roo presumed the person was a local Islamic scholar or an authoritative imam. After hanging up, the lecturer said the person would call back. In two minutes the phone rang, and after a brief conversation, the lecturer hung up and turned to converse in the local language with the other men. Finally, he said, "Abu Roo, we have concluded that 'khalifah' means 'a representative for someone who has died.'"

Abu Roo was intrigued by this response and said, "Wait a minute. Are you telling me that Allah is dead?"

Abu Roo watched the blood drain from their faces as his friends excitedly turned to talk with each other again. After a moment they announced once more, "We must call!"

Three and a half hours and 15 phone calls later, the group was only halfway through the first study.

For the last two years, Abu Roo and his small multi-agency team have continued to conduct holy book studies like this with devout Muslims. Although many of those who come to these studies can recite Quranic verses from memory faster than a computer can pull them up, Abu Roo and his team have seen tremendous fruit in studying the Quran and Bible side-by-side with their Muslim friends. Many who have attended these studies have grown fascinated with the person of Isa al Masih. They have willingly and eagerly investigated God's message in the other holy books – the Torah, Psalms, and Injil. Already, more than twenty Muslims have chosen to follow Isa al Masih as they have studied these books together.

The team Abu Roo participates with has also had the opportunity to train others in the use of the Seven Signs study. Another group of Christian workers in the same area operates an English training centre that has attracted about 1,000 students a year for the last 10 years, but they had never seen any of their students put their faith in Jesus. Within two years of receiving training from Abu Roo's team, they've already seen three of their students choose to follow Isa, with several others actively seeking truth through an on-going Bible study.

Abu Roo admits he's learned a lot of lessons along the way. That first study, for example, taught him two important lessons. The first came from the phone calls. Abu Roo wondered why his friends couldn't answer a simple question ("What does khalifah mean?"). When they made their phone calls, he wondered why the person on the other end couldn't answer right away. Why did he always have to call back in a few minutes? Abu Roo discovered that even though his friends were well-versed in Islamic tradition and the Quran, they were not comfortable interpreting even the simplest words in the Quran for themselves. They were conditioned to seek an answer from someone of higher authority. Apparently, so was the one they called.

In Islam, concluded Abu Roo, young people develop impressive skills reciting the Quran, but they're not trained to interpret what they've read. They're taught to go to some other source or authority for interpretation. "They know only what someone else tells them the Quran says or means," he says. "Even though they can recite huge parts of it, they don't really know what it says. Our study forces them to look at black ink on white paper to really come to grips with what their book says, as well as what the Bible says. We have found this to be very powerful."

As a result, Abu Roo and his team realize the importance of teaching seekers and new believers how to examine the text for themselves. "A good place to begin," he says, "is to open the Injil to Matthew 5 to study the Sermon on the Mount. In so doing, we teach our friends to ask simple questions. Who is speaking? Why is he speaking? To whom is he speaking? Where is he speaking? What is he trying to teach? And finally, how does this apply to my life today?"

When the seekers or believers learn to answer these questions, they learn to unlock the meaning of the text for themselves. "This has been revolutionary," says Abu Roo.

Early on, after Abu Roo taught a young student to study the holy books like this, the young man ran up to him one day and said, "Abu Roo, I just read 300 pages of the Injil last week!"

"He read so much," asserts Abu Roo, "because it became alive to him. He was finally able to say, 'This is speaking to me, personally, and I can learn and understand truth without having to go to somebody else to find out what it means.'"

From this and other experiences, Abu Roo's team has learned the value of not only leading their Muslim friends to the holy books, but also teaching them how to discover for themselves the truths these books contain.

Abu Roo has also learned that the studies have even more impact when someone from a Muslim background leads them. He says, "For me, a Westerner, trying to tell someone else what the Quran says is a major hurdle to get over." He's seen that believers who come from a Muslim background lead the studies with far more effectiveness. They also help Abu Roo and his team mates understand how to adjust their studies to make them more contextually relevant and understandable to the people from this country.

Abu Roo and his team encourage their friends to begin leading studies very early in their spiritual journey. In weekly holy book studies, they look for participants who could lead discussions. They will tell the person, "OK, Abdullah, next week you must come prepared to lead the discussion on the next five verses. You need to read and study these verses, asking the questions, 'Who?', 'What?', 'When?', 'Where?', 'Why?', and 'How does it apply to me?' Be prepared to answer these questions for us and to lead our discussion."

Abu Roo and the team look for individuals who have the potential to lead and act to get them involved quickly. Even if they are still seekers and have not yet come to faith in Jesus, they will be encouraged to lead the next study.

How can Abu Roo's team ask a "non-believer" to lead a discussion about spiritual truths? It's because of a fundamental principle that under girds their approach. They concentrate on discipleship, not conversion.

The Seven Signs study emphasizes this approach. Abu Roo explains that there are other methods of studying the Quran alongside the Bible, but many of these start where their study ends. "We try to lay a foundation that tracks to Jesus, as opposed to putting him out there at the front – an approach which is often a source of contention to Muslims who don't even understand what their own book says about him."

Abu Roo points out that in the Great Commission itself, Jesus puts the emphasis on making disciples. "As you go and make disciples, you're teaching them the truths and principles Jesus taught, while leaving conversion as a mysterious work of the Holy Spirit." Rebirth comes from the Spirit, Abu Roo says, referring to John 3:3-8.

Abu Roo's team emphasizes this pattern in their work. He says, "In contrast to the West, where we seek 'a decision,' then may or may not effectively disciple a person, we endeavour to do the discipleship up front. We trust that a person will come to genuine faith after being taught truth."

The term "conversion" is not a word Abu Roo and his team choose to use in describing a Muslim who has come to faith in Jesus. In the context of their part of the world, "conversion" implies abandonment of the God of Abraham in favour of three gods, acceptance of the West's hedonistic and immoral lifestyle, and abandonment of one's family, tribe, culture and heritage. Such an act is considered worthy of death. Abu Roo says, "We're not trying to Christianise anybody, but we are trying to help them have a personal and vital relationship with the living God."

Abu Roo does not have a problem with a Muslim background believer considering Muhammad a prophet. Most likely, he says, the person first heard the name of Isa al Masih through Muhammad. Nor does he have a problem with a person attending a local mosque, reading the Quran, praying five times a day, or using the term "Muslim" to describe his or her identity. "I think what is important is a person being surrendered to the lordship of Jesus Christ," Abu Roo says, mentioning Matthew 7:21-23. "I believe the Word of God and the Holy Spirit of God are fully capable of giving direction in a person's life. This is true especially if that person has been or is in the active process of being discipled. I do not feel I must tell a person to completely abandon their culture and choose mine in order for them to follow Christ."

While he believes it is possible for a person to follow Jesus Christ within the cultural context of Islam, Abu Roo is adamantly opposed to syncretism. "Islam considers one thing to be heretical, and that is to leave Islam," he asserts. "You can actually believe all kinds of different and contradictory things in Islam, like animism and spiritism. You can certainly believe in Isa's virgin birth, his prophethood, messiahship, that he is the Word of God, the Spirit of God, that he is the mercy of God and the Grace of God, and that he is alive today in heaven waiting to return to judge the earth. All of these things are in the Quran. What is not taught to Muslims is the truth and purpose of Christ's substitutionary death and resurrection."

Abu Roo says he and his team look for evidence of the Holy Spirit changing the lives of their friends. "What I want is for my Muslim friends to have a real encounter with Jesus. How can anyone ever be the same after that? As long as they're not practicing or believing something contrary to what Jesus taught, I'm not going to be picky about how it may compare with my Western Christian traditions. I think this is one of the applications we can make from the decision of the Jerusalem council in Acts 15."

Again, Abu Roo and his team do not emphasize "conversion" in the traditional understanding of the term. If a believer from a Muslim background wants to follow Western Christian traditions, they will simply ask, "What's the best way for you to reach your family and loved ones? If, because of their ignorance, your family perceives you as having abandoned God, your culture, your tribe, family and heritage, will you be able to effectively share the truths of Isa with them? Does it open a door of opportunity, or does it permanently close it?"

When a person has the freedom to explore truth while staying within the Islamic culture, Abu Roo's team finds that the Bible powerfully speaks to those who study it. They are careful to try not to talk people into anything, but to let God speak to them. "My pastor back home," recalls Abu Roo, "always used to say, 'Anything you talk somebody into, someone else can come along and talk them out of.' We want to be guides to truth, but we don't want to tell somebody what to believe."

They let the Holy Spirit speak through the pages of the Bible, and at the same time, they also let him speak through friendships. Abu Roo's team actively encourages Muslim seekers of

Isa to develop friendships with each other. They realize that truth comes to their friends in many forms, not just through the studies themselves. Informal discussion is one of those forms. Although a Seven Signs study may begin as a one-on-one dialog between one of Abu Roo's team and a friend they've made, the team member quickly seeks to introduce his or her friend to the wider circle of seekers and believers.

In the beginning, some who attend the holy book studies express reluctance to meet others. To counter these fears, the team tries to make the introductions as non-threatening and fun as possible. They find any excuse to throw a party or to have a gathering of friends. It might be someone's birthday, a student may have received a good grade on an exam or a family member may have come to visit. Almost any excuse is a good reason to host a gathering.

At the event, a seeker may find himself in conversation with an intellectual believer who has memorized the Quran and who comes from an Islamic background. He can quote from memory verses from the Quran that support scripture and his faith in Isa.

Abu Roo has found that many of the believers they know speak boldly of their faith in Isa al Masih. They say, "Yes, I'm a Muslim, but what does 'Muslim' mean? It means to be surrendered to God. Isa is the one who taught me how to be surrendered to God. The Quran is the book that introduced me to Isa and told me to read the Injil, the Torah, and the Psalms. I've done that and come to a fuller understanding of what it means to be Muslim. Let me share with you why Isa is so important and why Muhammad talked about him."

All told, Abu Roo and his team engage in several types of outreach meetings: Seven Signs studies for individual seekers, regular social gatherings to develop trust and friendship, weekly one-on-one discipleship with individual believers, and when possible, a monthly group Bible study. Any believer or seeker may attend, and they're welcome to bring their friends.

Often Abu Roo's team finds that as people begin to read all the holy books, and as they meet people who share their interest in knowing more about Allah, somewhere along the way they encounter the living God. It doesn't seem to matter what people may think of the Bible when they first begin to read it. They may believe it is of lesser importance than the Quran, or that it has been corrupted. "In our experience," says Abu Roo, "in a very short period of time as we proceed to read through the Quran and the Bible together, the Quran just seems to fade in importance. It just steps aside and the Bible becomes relevant."

With that confidence, Abu Roo never feels the need to defend or argue for the authority of scripture. He says, "If you really believe that the Word of God is living and powerful, and sharper than any two-edged sword, piercing to the division of soul and spirit, and of joints and marrow, and is a discerner of the thoughts and intents of the heart, then why would anyone need to defend it? We simply need to say, 'Let's just look at what it says and you can judge for yourself.'"

Abu Roo says, "At some point in the process of teaching basic spiritual truths, a person is going to wake up one day and say, 'Now I get it! I am a follower of Isa al Masih. I have a changed life, and I now understand the significance of Isa's sacrifice and I know he is my saviour.' When this happens, it's not just lip service; it's something that God has done. The power of his Word and the power of his Holy Spirit come together just as scripture tells us it does, and he transforms that person's life."

For many who have attended Seven Signs studies led by Abu Roo's team, that moment of realization often happens before they even reach the study of the last sign. It is not uncommon for that light to turn on during the second or third study. Alternatively, this is also often the point at which some people abandon the study.

Others reach the conclusion of the study and find themselves facing a major decision: "What am I going to do with Isa al Masih?" At this point, the members of Abu Roo's team encourage the person to go to God himself in prayer to find out what he wants them to do about this man called Isa al Masih.

Abu Roo recalls one man, Rahman, who came to this point and faced this hard decision. The team members meeting with Rahman didn't try to force him or lead him in a specific prayer of contrition or confession. They simply said, "OK Rahman, what do you think God wants you to do?"

Rahman answered, "I don't know. I don't know if I should accept Christ or not, or if I should even believe this. You know I'm a Muslim, and what you've told me is so contrary to everything I've ever been taught."

The team members replied, "Well, why don't you just ask God what you should do? Ask Allah and let him, not us, tell you what to believe."

So, they knelt down on the floor together and prayed with Rahman, asking Allah to give their friend understanding as to what he needed to do. After a few minutes of prayer and being still before God, they asked him, "Did God speak to you?"

Rahman said, "No."

They asked, "Well, did you see anything? Did Allah give you a vision?"

He said, "Yes, I see something right now."

"What do you see?"

Rahman answered, "I see Isa standing in the corner across the room."

They asked, "What's he doing?"

"He's standing there with his arms open."

"What do you think he wants?"

"I think he wants me to come to him."

"So, what are you going to do?"

"I think I need to pray."

"We think that's a good idea."

Then the team mates, after weeks of study and countless hours of prayer for Rahman, received the precious gift of sharing in their friend's prayer.

Abu Roo recalls, "He placed his face to the ground. Then, without being guided or lead, he prayed out loud the most beautiful prayer of contrition and confession that anyone could ever put pen to paper to write out. He asked Isa al Masih to be his saviour and Lord."

What had begun with a sign had led Rahman to the saviour.

After four years as an assistant magazine editor, CJ Daniel has spent 15 years working in communications with a large international agency. He's currently writing a book about people who follow Jesus but don't call themselves Christians. If you are interested in being trained to use the Seven Signs study, please write to sevensigns1@yahoo.com.

Desperate Enough to Pray

by EJ Martin

"Father, move on Abu Yusuf! Grant him a sign to confirm who Jesus is." On the roof of the house where he lived with a local family, Owen Campbell called out all night for God to reveal himself. Though he had lived with Abu Yusuf's family for only a few months, Owen sensed that God was stirring the man's heart. Owen's brother Samuel, visiting from abroad, joined him for that night of powerful prayer, when they sensed they were encountering spiritual powers at work around them.

Owen recalls, "We had such an intense night of spiritual warfare. I know some people regularly have spiritual insight about 'powers,' but I'm not that kind of guy! Weird things were happening around the house—even with animals in the area. Yet we felt compelled to keep on praying for God to give a sign to Abu Yusuf."

At Christmas a week earlier, Owen had thrown a "Jesus Party" for a dozen friends in the neighbourhood. The mother of the house had kindly cooked food, and after the meal, Owen put the JESUS film into the video player. After everyone else had left, Abu Yusuf said, "Rewind the tape. I want to watch it again."

Seven days later, Owen says, "It seemed that Abu Yusuf was ready to make a commitment to Jesus. We just needed to make a clear invitation. So Samuel and I asked him, 'Why don't you follow Jesus?'"

Abu Yusuf responded, "I'm interested, but I want you to pray for a sign."

So the brothers sat beside him and prayed, asking God to confirm to Abu Yusuf that he should follow Jesus. Then as Abu Yusuf climbed into bed, they climbed the steps to the roof to begin what became their night-long vigil. Finally, just before the morning call to prayer, the sense of intensity lessened. Feeling God's peace, they crawled into bed in Owen's room.

Within a few hours, Abu Yusuf was a pounding on the door. "I couldn't sleep all night!"

The brothers shot a conspiratorial glance at each other that said, "OK! It wasn't just us, then!"

Abu Yusuf continued, "At about the morning call to prayer, I finally fell asleep. Immediately, I had a dream. There was a knock on the door and when I opened it, Jesus was standing there.

"He said to me, 'May I come in? Would you make some supper for me?' So I made some lentils. I was just about to feed him when he said, 'Wait a minute. There's someone else coming.' So we waited, and there was a knock on the door and it was a neighbour. I invited him in and was about to feed him when Jesus said, 'No, wait.' There was another knock on the door and there were two or three more neighbours.

"Eventually, there was a line out into the street, and I said, 'Jesus, I can't feed them all!'

"Jesus said, 'That's OK. Just start serving.' And it was amazing! I started serving and there was enough for everyone! And then I woke up. But I fell right back to sleep and had the exact same dream a second time!"

Owen asked, "What happened then?"

"I was tired because I hadn't slept all night. So I fell asleep a third time. And guess what! I had the exact same dream a third time!

"Now I'm knocking on your door. I want to do the water thing tonight."

Owen was excited by this man's eagerness for baptism, thinking, "Wow! This is powerful! And it was so easy!"

This experience laid for Owen a clear foundation about the power of prayer. He thought to himself, "At this rate, within ten years the whole country will be following Jesus and we'll move on to the next country."

Owen had moved to this Middle Eastern city when he was 21, spent a year studying Arabic, and then found other expatriates who felt God had called them to show Jesus' love to the poor in their predominantly Muslim city. He joined their team, living with them in a slum.

Quite a lot seemed to happen in a hurry. Within his first few days in Abu Yusuf's house, discussions turned spiritual. Owen, still knowing very little Arabic, had brought his new team leader to meet the household when Abu Yusuf admitted, "I drink alcohol all the time, and I can't stop."

Owen's team leader replied, "Why don't we pray, and you can have that addiction broken."

Abu Yusuf said, "You could get all the Christians from your countries together, and nothing would ever change, because that's my fate. It's written upon me that I'll be an alcoholic."

"Well, don't you worry. It's really easy. We'll just pray for you in the name of Isa al Masih that you'll stop. Is that OK?"

"Whatever. That's fine."

"OK, great! Owen will pray for you."

Photo credit: iStockPhoto.com

This was a surprise to Owen! He spoke very little Arabic at the time, but he somehow spluttered out a prayer that must have sounded remotely right.

The team began to pray for their neighbourhood with fresh passion. Owen wasn't from a church background that taught him about hearing God speak. But he began to get the sense that they should pray about certain issues to do with the spiritual state and the predominant sins within their neighbourhood.

Then Abu Yusuf put his faith in Jesus Christ, and in the next couple of months, a few more in the neighbourhood did too. His team also heard exciting stories from others in their city that a few Muslims were beginning to follow Jesus. No wonder Owen thought it was all going to be easy.

Of course it didn't happen quite like that ...

Like most of the countries in the region where Jesus walked the earth, this one has an ancient Christian population. But when Owen moved there, he had quickly discovered that virtually none of the local Christians shared his sense of responsibility to tell their Muslim neighbours how much Jesus loves them.

Shortly after his encounter with Abu Yusuf, he met a local Christian woman named Mona who did share that sense of responsibility. She started visiting the neighbourhood where the team lived. Owen thought to himself, "This is radical! Here is a local Christian girl who is willing to wearing a scarf to be appropriate in the community." Within a few years, Owen and Mona married. As newlyweds, the Campbells continued to reach out to Muslim neighbours.

But this brief period of fruitfulness came to a dramatic halt. They almost felt as though God said, "OK, now that I've got your heart on board, let's see how you persevere without any fruit. Are you really excited about me? Or are you excited about the fruit?" They felt as though a tap had been turned off.

For the next 10 years, they knew almost no one who put faith in Christ. In fact, Abu Yusuf fell away from Christ. Though they held on with faith that God was still at work in their city, the years dragged on.

Meanwhile, they served in a local national church. Eventually the leadership of the church gave them their blessing to form teams to reach Muslims, saying, "Take our best people. If they want to work with you, pull them out of whatever else they're doing."

A handful of people joined Owen and Mona for weekly meetings, fellowship, prayer and training in apologetics. But they got nowhere. After three years of frustration, the Campbells decided to pull the plug on the effort. On the night they announced the dissolution of the team, one man said, "I'm really upset! I mean, I know that I haven't even talked to a Muslim for more than a year, but at least coming here every week made me feel guilty about it."

Owen and Mona weren't seeing any fruit either. Nothing was working. They looked back on those first few years and asked themselves, "Why did that period of fruitfulness stop? What did we start to do differently? What's wrong with us? ... God, what are we doing in this country?"

In that place of extreme barrenness, they turned to prayer – not for any noble reasons, but simply because they had no other options left.

Throughout the next year, the Campbells were stirred in a strange way for their city. "It took the shape of ..." Owen breaks off, groping for the best words to describe his experience. "It was strange stuff. In the late afternoons, I would start to feel 'down.' By late evening, I would actually feel like crying. Grief washed over me every day, usually peaking at about midnight. I stayed up crying until about one o'clock every morning." The late nights of grieving and crying continued for about six months, and they started to understand that their grief reflected God's heart for their city.

As they pored over scripture, prayed, talked with others, and followed some hunches, the Campbells felt God leading them to study their city's spiritual dynamics and history through three paths. With a new group of expatriate team members, they eventually classified these paths into their "Three Rs": research, relationship, and revelation. This process led them to identify several "strongholds," as the Campbells came to call them. These strongholds were a result of specific patterns of sin, and people's tendencies to commit the patterns of sin reinforced those same strongholds.

Idolatry. One of the earliest established strongholds, these idols were actual spiritual beings with which people made alliances. "They gave allegiance to and got benefits from them," Owen says. The effects seemed to continue through the centuries, in the country's pagan, Christian and Muslim eras. "For example, we see this idolatry in modern patterns of leadership, where leaders are still honoured almost as king-gods. This existed in early Christian monastic movements as well as in Muslim patterns. It even affects current church leadership."

Obsession with death. Legalism and fear, he says, are entangled with the rituals related to death in his country, from earliest recorded history until today.

Magic. Overt practices of magic have long been part of the culture, and some are still exercised in festivals or folk religion gatherings today. Many magic rituals and traditions are still a part of the lives of families and individuals, whether Muslim or Christian. All of these involve tapping into unseen spiritual power.

Oppression and injustice. Over the years, these have taken the forms of officially sanctioned sodomy and slavery. Additionally, cannibalism was practiced on a wide scale at several points in recorded history. Today, in this perpetual police state, the poor are exploited and those with no power are crushed. "What does it mean when your community lives under this kind of injustice for centuries? There are all kinds of implications," Owen says.

A specific approach to Islam. Owen calls this the "youngest" of the strongholds, dating back not to the beginning of Islam, but "only" to the 10th century. At that time, Muslim leaders established an institution that promoted a specific brand of Islam that has given birth to some of the most violent and fundamentalist strains of Islamic thinking today.

In order to identify these strongholds, the team became students of the city's history by searching online and in libraries, and by studying the historical monuments still scattered around the cityscape. They began to identify recurring patterns of sin throughout the city's millennia of history. "We discovered legal alliances, ratified by leaders in the community with specific gods or powers or spirit beings, and wondered about the residual effect of those alliances," says Owen. "We saw that the same main sins recurred century after century in different forms."

The second means they used to investigate the spiritual dynamics of the city was to see whether they could find evidence of the strongholds in the context of current relationships. The team compiled a long list of standard "rejection lines" that people would use when hearing about Jesus. They found clear connections between most of these rejection lines and the strongholds of sin. Two examples:

The response of idolatry. Muslims often responded, "What you say about Jesus is really great; it grabs my heart. But my leader (or father, or the imam that I'm following) totally disagrees. I can't take a step without his approval. Jesus sounds beautiful. But he's not my leader." Christians responded similarly when challenged to share the gospel with Muslim neighbours, saying, "My pastor would never allow it."

The response of witchcraft: Muslims would reject the good news by saying, "If I do what you're saying, I'll fall under the powers of darkness." Even a new believer, as he was being trained in his faith, once told a team member, "All that stuff you're teaching me from the Bible is really great, but you know, there are other ways of finding out things about God, too. If we go into a closed room and chant a certain phrase over and over again, an angel will appear to us and tell us secrets."

The final means of clarifying the spiritual dynamics of the city was that God spoke to them through direct revelation. Owen recalls, "God communicated to us in many ways, including words of prophecy or words of knowledge, 'burdens' that we or others felt, and a sense of agreement with others in prayer. In addition, over the course of two years, people from around the world ended up in our living room, saying, 'God has told us to come here and pray for this country. We have some specific pieces of information that we feel we need to tell you.' And what they said lined up with what we were discovering about these strongholds through research and relationship."

As a counterpoint to each of the strongholds, they sensed that God wanted to call forth its opposite; for example, they felt that instead of idolatry, God was calling forth worship from their country. "Of course, God invites worship from everywhere," says Owen. "But it seemed as though this would be a key to seeing the breakthrough that God wanted to bring to our city. Over the years, this 'calling forth' has become the most significant part of what God has revealed to us about breaking strongholds."

Additionally, says Owen, each of the strongholds seemed to have "spirit powers that were assigned by the enemy to defend and nurture these areas of sin. In prayer, we focused on asking the Father for these powers to be bound so that strongholds could be broken and truth proclaimed with clarity."

Meanwhile, other Christian leaders and small circles of believers were beginning to pray for their country with fresh intensity. "In retrospect," says Owen, "I see that God was sovereignly starting up a prayer movement that was going to gain a lot of momentum. No one knew it at the time. No one owned it. It wasn't anyone's bright idea." Some, like the Campbells, had turned to prayer out of desperation, others simply because they were convinced from scripture that this was what God wanted. Eventually, about a dozen of these national prayer leaders connected with each other and agreed to begin to pray together. A man named Samir emerged as an accepted leader of the growing movement.

For years, a few faithful souls had held an annual prayer meeting for the country. Usually a few hundred people attended. Starting around the beginning of 2000, Samir and the other prayer leaders sent the word through the Christian community, calling believers to a fresh initiative in prayer. They were excited to see several hundred people attend a three-day prayer meeting.

By 2005, this meeting had exploded into an annual four-day fasting and prayer event with 10,000 people in attendance!

What happened? Owen looks back and sees God's sovereign orchestration. "At the right time, when nobody could claim it as their own, God raised up a leader who pulled everyone together." Weren't the government authorities suspicious about these large meetings? "The government allows them because they're harmless, 'Oh these Christian get-togethers, no big deal.' They had no idea. We had no idea!"

In the 2000 meeting, Samir invited the Campbells to talk about what they had been learning through their "Three Rs" of research, relationship and revelation. On that night, with fear and trembling, they began to talk about the strongholds God had showed them. They talked about God's love for the whole nation, not just for the Christian population. They reminded people of God's intention for those who are blessed to be a blessing to others.

By the time they finished, the believers across the room were on their knees in repentance. "Clearly, God had wanted to say something. As soon as we started speaking, it resonated in people's spirits. What a memorable night!" With tears glinting in his eyes at the memory, Owen recalls, "They cried out to God, repenting of having abandoned spiritual care of their land."

Mona continues, "As an oppressed minority, you don't want to attract attention. You just want to preserve yourself. Keep your kids safe. Just survive. ... That night, they began to hear God say, 'You are not just to survive. You are to take your place as my royal priesthood. You intercede. You stand up, because you're the children of the king.' It was such a shift in identity."

Today, the annual four-day prayer event is just the tip of a wide prayer movement. Networks of about 150 leaders across the country are training others to pray strategically for their country. "There were people praying before, but it was nothing compared to now," says Owen. "There was this real sense of ignition in the early years of the new millennium. Boom! Suddenly, a new prayer movement was on the scene, orchestrated by God."

As the annual prayer meetings grew and local networks of prayer sprang up across the country, the Campbells noticed a simultaneous "temperature change" in Christians' attitudes toward Muslims – from antagonism, to fear, to a tentative openness for Muslims to hear the gospel "from other people, but not from me."

In retrospect, Owen can now identify several stages of prayer as God brought people's hearts into line with his. As people carry on in prayer, their prayers change, he says.

Before the prayer movement ignited, the oppressed minority prayed: "O God, have mercy on us. Rescue us from those bad Muslims who persecute us."

Then as they caught sight of a vision that their whole land could be touched by the good news about Jesus, prayers turned victorious: "God, move across our land, and show the Muslims that we were right all along."

One night in 2001, Owen and a team mate were invited to talk about prayer to about 30 young adults. In the past, he had sat through countless prayer meetings while many prayed with tepid faith: "O Lord, maybe someday you might do a little bit in our country."

"But at this meeting," he recalls, "when we told them that God had called us here to bless Muslims, they surged around us, laid hands on us, and prayed: 'O God, pour out your power. Move on our land!' Their prayers revealed a tangibly different faith."

Those who continued to pray found their hearts changing and praying: "O God, so much of our land is Muslim. And you love them, not just us." In the 2002 prayer conference, with tears in their eyes, participants streamed toward the altar to acknowledge publicly that they felt God calling them to pray specifically for Muslims or to reach out in love. Instead of being a rarity, it began to be commonplace to hear of Christians who wanted to share Jesus with Muslims.

Those who persisted in prayer, says Owen, increased in "Acts 4 boldness. We're hearing about more and more people starting to share their faith with Muslims. I mean, you can't even count it any more. I remember being able to count on one hand the people who were sharing their faith with Muslims. But now there's no way to keep track!"

A growing number of Christians are not simply sharing their faith casually with neighbours and colleagues, but they are intentionally focusing their lives around helping Muslims follow Jesus. Yacoub, a local believer, has spent more than a decade on his own in prayer for and outreach to the Muslims of his country. For years, he longed to see others share his burden. The answer to his longing came out of the prayer movement, starting in earnest in around 2005. Today, Yacoub oversees about 40 people in four cities – local believers who've connected to this purpose because of the prayer movement. A few of them are being supported by their churches; most work to support themselves but focus their free time on outreach. Week by week, they tell fresh stories of Muslims putting faith in Christ.

For the last few summers, Yacoub and others have run a three-week school to train 15-20 believers to share their faith. Most of the trainees are from a Christian background, but a few believers from Muslim background have joined the school as well. In 2008, a 21-year-old woman attended. After spending afternoons sharing her faith in cafés and at parties, she concluded, "I'm giving my life to this. I want nothing else. I just want to do God's will."

Mona recalls that locally composed contemporary worship songs have reflected the same shift in emphasis as prayers have. "I have clear memories of the mourning songs we sang when I was a girl: 'O Lord, turn to me. Have mercy on me. Why are you abandoning me?' Now we have entered a period of faith and hope-filled joy in our worship. The reality of what's happening out there on the streets hasn't shifted.

People are still oppressed. But at these prayer conferences, people are dancing with joy because they're so full of faith and hope about what God is going to do in our land."

The Campbells see these new expressions of worship in the context of "clear instruction from God about the first stronghold of idolatry and the corresponding need to call forth worship within our city. You can call it all a coincidence, call it whatever you want. We don't really care how it happened. But God alerted us to call forth certain things and all of a sudden, in the space of a few years, we've seen a great shift that has changed the whole perspective."

This great shift in prayer has not only affected Christians' willingness to witness, but also Muslims' receptivity. "We see more softness and openness and questioning all over the place. There has been an atmosphere change among Muslims," says Owen.

He finds that Muslims are now regularly having dreams and visions of Jesus. One day, Owen hailed a taxi as he was leaving a church wedding. The festivities had left him tired, not interested in talking to anyone. "But something inside me was saying that this Muslim taxi driver had had a vision of Jesus. Was this a word of knowledge? I don't … I'm not … I don't get these things … that often." He gropes for the right way to describe his experience.

"So I said, Oooooooh-Kaaaay God …"

Swallowing hard, after a few words of greeting, he jumped right in, asking the driver, "Have you, by any chance, ever had a dream or vision of Jesus?"

They talked for two hours about the vision of Jesus the man had as a teenager. "He didn't make a decision to follow Jesus, but it was so just easy to share with him.

"And my experience is not an isolated story. Within Yacoub's team, they tell fresh stories of new believers every week. It's now happening regularly. They say, 'We sent a team out and they met a girl. She had had dreams of Jesus. We talked with her, and now she's a new believer. Isn't that great?' " In the last few years, Yacoub's team members are meeting more Muslims who have already secretly come to faith in Jesus through the witness of satellite television or correspondence courses. They help to connect these new believers with others.

Owen tells the story of Hamdy (a follower of Jesus from Islam) and George (a Christian background believer) caught a taxi together. Noting the Quran on the dashboard that identified the driver as a Muslim, Hamdy said to him, "Can you believe these Christians? You won't believe what he thinks about God." He indicated George. "Can you believe that he thinks that Jesus is the way that God gives us to be saved from hell? He thinks that Jesus actually knows and cares for each of us." Hamdy went on to talk about Jesus.

The driver responded, "Wow! Are you serious? Do they really believe that?"

Then Hamdy invited George, "Tell him about it!"

The driver parked his taxi and the three men talked for two hours. In time, the driver became the leader of a fellowship of believers, and his wife also put her faith in Jesus.

"This cooperation between believers from Muslim and Christian backgrounds is revolutionary from the local church point of view," says Owen. "The church is not trying to own the new believers. They're allowing them to form their own fellowships with their own leadership and their own cultural norms that match their culture more closely."

For years, Christians working with Muslims have employed code words to talk about their activities. To cloak their meanings, many would say things like, "We're working with the majority." Or, "... with the friends." But Owen says the first time he met some of Yacoub's team members, they told him, with a shout for emphasis, "We're working with Muslims!" Their boldness surprised him, so they explained, "When we say it that way, it breaks the spirit of fear inside of us."

The inevitable backlash has resulted. Yacoub has been questioned and threatened by governmental authorities. A newspaper has published a story saying that he is trying to convert Muslims to Christianity. (The authorities often deal with those they consider troublemakers by stirring up others to attack them.)

The Campbells say they sense God leading them to pray specifically for 12 more men like Yacoub to be raised to disciple and train new believers and team leaders.

In addition to backlash and persecution, the small groups of new believers also struggle against the lingering effects of sin. A woman professes faith in Christ but shows no evidence of a changed life. A married leader of a house church shows romantic interest in a single woman in the fellowship, and the fledgling church disintegrates.

Despite the backlash, persecution and set-backs, Christians who have been changed by the prayer movement are starting to move to other Arabic-speaking countries in order to share what they've experienced. No central church structure is coordinating them. "They're just going!" says Mona.

In the last few years, the Campbells have begun to study what God is doing through prayer in other countries. "Across the Muslim world today," he says, "we see three main strands of prayer: local people from a Christian background, sent-in workers, and local people from a Muslim background. In each, God is raising up prayer in a new way." They are coordinating their prayer efforts with others worldwide in a group of people who are committed to "prayer for the Muslim world from within the Muslim world."

Owen points out that Acts 6:4 defines the work of apostles as the ministry of the word and of prayer. Both. "Obviously, the ministry of the word gets incarnated by people going and living among and learning language and speaking the word of God. ... Prayer, which is that same apostolic work, needs to happen in the same incarnational way. You go, you live there, and you pray from inside the place." He pauses to think carefully and names eight other Muslim-majority countries as "places where there's been a clear, tangible link between prayer and a significant push forward in establishing communities of Jesus followers."

"It's exactly what happens when you connect with God consistently on a deep level," say Owen. "God says, 'Good. Whoosh!' " He fans out his fingers to demonstrate how God is whooshing people out into other countries. "All this has been borne out of the prayer movement. Other factors helped, but nothing really ignited until sustained, intentional, focused prayer called it forth."

EJ Martin once lived in the Campbells' country and has often prayed for its people. Contact the Campbells at IS56.12345678@gmail.com.

The Messiah Is Not a Liar

by Eric Adams

The young man paused, bowed slightly, and came to shake the hand of the old man sitting in the quiet shade of the thatched roof overhang. "Hello, shaykh," the youth said. The old man looked up and smiled.

"Please sit," the elder said, waving to the worn brick stoop on his right. On the side of the house, chickens pecked in the dust. A woman arrived with a pail of water on her head and walked into the back of the two-room house.

Other men and women drifted up to the front of the house and also greeted the shaykh. With much shaking of hands, each new arrival greeted everyone else before sitting on the mats in front of the house. Women pooled into the left side of the courtyard, men on the right. A quiet murmur flowed among them, punctuated by soft exclamations ("*Eeyai?!*" "*Eeeh!*") as they exchanged news of families, crops, and the life of the village.

Then the village leaders began to arrive – the religious leader from the mosque, the village chief, and his assistant. They greeted the shaykh and others in the small crowd then sat in the three chairs set aside for them in the shade of the tree.

Slowly they all quieted, like the dust settling around them on the red earth. They looked toward the shaykh expectantly, and he began to lead them in prayers, his palms open to receive the blessing of God falling on them. The men and women also opened their hands for the blessing. As the shaykh finished praying, they all lifted their hands to their faces and many quietly said, "Praise be to God, amen."

After a moment's silence, a woman spoke. "Shaykh, Noora has a story to tell about what happened after you taught us about the Samaritan last week." The old man looked towards Noora.

"Shaykh, I was riding my bicycle back to my village after the last teaching," Noora started, "and I saw a crowd gathered at the bridge. They were looking over the embankment toward the river. A woman told me that a young man on a bicycle had missed the road and fallen down the embankment. But no one was doing anything! I remembered that in the story, the priest and Levite walked on the other side of the road to avoid the injured Samaritan. The people in the crowd at the bridge were just like those religious people. I realized that Isa al Masih would want me to be like the Samaritan, so I climbed down the bank and helped the young man back to the road. I gave him to someone from his village who would help him get home."

The old man smiled, "Noora has showed us an important example! It is not enough to listen to the stories of the messiah. We must act on what he teaches us. The Samaritan story teaches us to show mercy, and that was what you did, daughter. It was a courageous thing. It was a good thing. Isa al Masih gives us the strength to do the right actions."

Musa, for this was the shaykh's name, pulled out a booklet, worn with use. "Today," he said, "we will talk about the prophet who was told by God to marry a prostitute!" A murmur of surprise rippled across his audience. "Yes, it is true!" the old teacher said with animation.

"This is a strange story. Hosea was a prophet, and one day the word of God came to him saying, 'Go and marry an adulteress, and conceive children of unfaithfulness!' What an amazing thing! Why did God ask him to do this? God asked

Photo credit: AIM-On Field Media

Hosea to do this terrible thing because God's people had become unfaithful to him, untrustworthy. Everyone knows that a prostitute cannot be trusted by anyone. God's people had become like this – untrustworthy. There was too much unfaithfulness."

"Shaykh, we have this problem too," admitted one man in the group. "There is unfaithfulness among our people. We are unfaithful in our use of money and food. We throw money away on useless things, and we eat all our food and do not prepare for the famine time."

"There is also unfaithfulness between husbands and wives," said a woman.

"Yes," Musa said, "marriages are fragile because of unfaithfulness between husbands and wives."

"And between people and their chiefs," said another man.

"Yes," Musa said, "People are not trustworthy. Broken trust is at the root of unfaithfulness."

"God gave children to Hosea and his prostitute wife, and God told Hosea to give them names like 'Not-Mercy' and 'Not-My-People' to tell his people that they were no longer people of God and they would not find mercy on the day of judgement. Just like Hosea's prostitute wife and the people of Israel, too many of us are unfaithful to God and each other. Even if we go to the mosque regularly and pray five times a day – if we are unfaithful to the trust people give us and unfaithful to the trust God has given us, he will reject us on the day of judgement."

Musa paused for a moment to give them a chance to register this solemn truth. Then he brightened, saying, "But there is hope. No matter how destructive and unfaithful we are, there is room for God to change us if we turn to him and allow him to change our hearts."

As Musa was talking, an old woman leaning on a staff arrived in front of the house and began to greet the women sitting the ground. Then she came and greeted Musa. "Hello, Shaykh," she said.

"Hello, Fatima," Musa answered.

Looking directly at him, she said, "I have a question."

"Ask, Mama," he says, using the respectful address for an older woman.

"What have you done to my husband?" Everyone looked at Fatima, her deeply wrinkled features flickering with both surprise and fear.

Musa said gently, "Is Haleem well, Mama?"

"Yes!" she said, as tracks of tears spilled down her cheeks. "Today, he got up, fed himself, and walked on his own!"

"Eeyai!" cried a woman called Aisha. "God has answered our prayers! Mama, he was here yesterday," she said. "He was with us, but he could only lie in the corner shaking with palsy. He couldn't move or get up without help." She added with embarrassment, "He even failed to help himself." Everyone understood that he couldn't even control his bladder.

"Yes," Fatima acknowledged. "He has been like that for this last year and a half."

Aisha continued to explain. "Yesterday, we had been talking about Hassan's wife – how God healed her from epilepsy. Nazeema and I were sitting across from your husband, and we said to him, 'Baba, you need to ask for prayer! You are always trembling and cannot do things for yourself.'

"He told us, 'It is only old age. Can we be cured of that?' But Nazeema and I pestered him until eventually he agreed to ask the group to pray for him. We told him he must destroy his charms and talismans. Haleem thought a moment then reluctantly agreed. Then several of the men gathered around him and prayed.'"

"I don't know about these prayers, but I do know that today he is changed! He is once again the man he was five years ago," the old wife said, tears dripping from her weathered chin.

The next day, two of the men who had heard Fatima's story were talking about Haleem's surprising improvement. Abdulla was a young man who had just begun coming to hear Musa tell these stories from the Bible. Paul was a foreigner who had been providing relief and agricultural training in the villages. Abdulla asked Paul what he thought of Fatima's tale of healing. Could it really be true? Paul suggested, "Why don't you go to Haleem's house and see for yourself?"

The youth jumped to his feet and began walking toward Haleem's house. On the path, he overtook Fatima, who had been shopping in a nearby village. He walked next to the old woman. "Come, Mama, I will walk back with you to see Haleem. Afterwards, I can tell the rest of the group what I have seen."

"Thank you, younger brother," the old woman said, looking at Abdulla as she shuffled along the road. Her eyes squinted with seriousness as she asked, "Do you really believe it was the prayers of the people in this group that changed my Haleem?"

"Mama, I am just learning about these things myself. We have been studying the life of Isa al Masih, learning how he healed many people. The people at this gathering prayed for Haleem in the name of Isa al Masih two days ago and now you say he has been healed. This is a wonder!"

"Should I pay the shaykh for this healing?"

Abdulla gazed out across the ragged fields of corn, much of it sickly from the scanty rains. A trio of women passed them with buckets of water on their heads. "No, I don't think so. He is not like the witch doctors. He always refuses to receive money, insisting that it's God who answers the prayer, not him."

"Really? Does this sort of thing happen often?" Fatima asked.

"There are many stories about Shaykh Musa and this gathering," Abdulla told her. "Once, a woman came to him and asked him to pray for her husband to return. The husband had been in South Africa for several years, but he came back within a week of the prayer. Another time, when Shaykh Musa was riding his bike, a spitting cobra blinded him. The people in the group prayed for him, and he could see again after a few days.

"The foreign teacher called Paul prays for people, too. So does his wife. She prayed for Hassan's wife and she was healed from epilepsy. And then there was the time that Shaykh Musa and the rest of the group prayed for a woman and her daughter who had epilepsy. Neither has had a seizure since."

Abdulla smiled. "There is a funny story, too. Once a neighbour's dog came and ate one of the shaykh's chickens. The shaykh confronted his neighbour and said, 'Your dog killed one of my chickens.' The neighbour shrugged it off. The shaykh asked him, 'Do you love your dog?' The neighbour didn't answer, so Shaykh Musa went home and prayed. The next day, the dog was dead. Everyone in the village was talking about that for months," he said with a laugh.

"Eeyai! There is power here!" the old woman said.

"Yes, but it's not like the power of the witch doctors. When Shaykh Musa and this group pray, they make people destroy the charms and talismans of the witch doctors. They say they must rely only on the power of God, not of spirits or men."

"When Haleem came home, he insisted on collecting all the charms that protect our health and our house. I wouldn't help him. It frightened me! But he took them outside and asked our neighbour to witness as he burned them."

They walked quietly together for a while, and then the woman asked, "Is the shaykh a Christian?"

Abdulla slowed as he thought, "No, Mama, I don't think so. At least he is not like those Christians in the church in our village. But he is not an unbeliever either! The shaykh has great joy in God, and he teaches us to be true followers of God in obedience. He is a follower of Isa al Masih, and he says that Isa has destroyed the power of sickness and sin – even death. That would be hard for me to believe if I hadn't heard the stories about Isa al Masih and seen the power of prayer in Isa's name. I begin to believe the shaykh is right."

They came to a hut showing signs of neglect and poverty. The old man sitting in front smiled as he saw his wife. "Hello, Baba," Abdulla said.

"Abdulla! Have you come to see what God has done?"

"Yes, Baba. The foreigner, Paul, sent me to see if it's true. Baba, can you stand on your own?"

"Yes, I can! Watch!" Haleem nimbly rose and sat back down in his chair by the wall of the house. "And I can get up again too," he said, rising to his feet.

"Baba, can you even sit on the ground?" asked the young man, amazed.

The old man sat on the red earth, then slowly rose again, smiling.

"Can you drink and feed yourself?"

Haleem laughed again and went into the house. He brought out a bit of corn porridge and ate it, and drank from a cup, his eyes twinkling. Abdulla laughed with him.

"Now tell me that there is a wildcat attacking my chickens!"

"Baba! There is a wildcat attacking your chickens!" Abdulla shouted.

The old man shambled out across the yard toward the chickens, shooing at the imaginary wildcat.

The three of them giggled at the silly antics. Abdulla wiped a tear from his eyes.

"Hello, Haleem." They turned. Ahmed, a neighbour, had come to see what was causing the commotion. Haleem walked into the house, picked up a heavy stump of wood, and brought it outside as a stool for his neighbour. Ahmed looked on, amazed.

"Haleem, my friend, how has this happened? You can even chase chickens, though I think the wildcat would be laughing on the ground." Abdulla and the old wife smiled.

"Ahmed, it was Shaykh Musa and his group. They prayed for me in the name of Isa al Masih, and look what has happened!"

"Musa!? Wasn't he the one you cared for during his initiation into manhood?"

Haleem nodded.

"And wasn't he the one we used to call 'Mr Profanity'? He was so angry and violent! And he has married and divorced so many times!"

Haleem nodded again. "God has changed him."

A few days later, Paul went to visit Shaykh Musa. They talked about Haleem's healing. It was late afternoon as they sat on the wooden porch in the shade of the tree. A few neighbours had begun to gather and sit around Paul and Musa to listen to their discussion.

After they discussed Haleem's new health for a long time, Musa said, "This is why I follow the messiah. He said, 'Whatever you ask for in my name, I will give it to you.' People come to me and ask for prayers. They come back again and say thanks for these answers to prayers.

"Yesterday, I went to see my friend Chingoli. He was lying in his bed and couldn't get up. He told me, 'I'm feeling much too cold. I don't know whether I'm going to live.'

"So I prayed in the name of the messiah, that the messiah would have mercy on him. Then I told him, 'Starting from today, you should sleep very well, and tomorrow you will come to my house. This will happen so that you will know that the messiah is working in you.'

"Today he came to see me here, and we had a nice long chat! In fact, he just left. He told me, 'Friend, today I am feeling much better. The answer to prayer, my renewed health, gives me faith that the messiah is not a liar.'

Musa continued, addressing the now significant group now around them, "I read in the Injil that before the messiah was born, an angel came to Maryam, mother of Isa. He told her that God had chosen her among all women. He said that what would be conceived within her would be the Word of God – from God himself. He said his word would create a baby in her. Of course, Maryam asked the angel how that could be possible since she had never been with a man before. The angel told her that it was possible because what God has said will not fail. He told her that the child would be a saviour, the one who would save all people."

As Musa talked, his quavering voice became animated. "If I reject Isa al Masih, aren't I rejecting God? Can I be following the true path if the Word of God comes to me and I reject him? If I reject the Word of God, then what word will I follow?

"When I began to understand the message about the messiah a few years ago, my heart was excited at the mention of God's will for us, so I had to follow that. And I love it!

"I have discovered that in following Isa al Masih I am following the laws of God and not of man. So I will surely follow him – without fear! He is the only one who came from heaven, proving it to us because people saw him go back to heaven. He is the only one who has risen from the dead. Isa al Masih is the only one who can show us what God is like.

"The messiah could heal the sick and raise people from the dead just by saying the word. Whatever the messiah said happened, and everyone saw it. His title, 'messiah,' means he was sent from God with work to do on the earth: to save us who are lost, to save us from hardship.

"The people who believe his word will have a big celebration, if we follow Isa al Masih with our whole hearts. When the day of judgement comes, we will be included among his people. We will be judged by him."

One of the bystanders asked, "Are you one of those who say Isa al Masih is the Son of God?"

Musa answered, "Isa said that because the authority of the Father has been given into his hands, he is granted the power to rule and judge. So doesn't that make him the Word of God?!

"In fact, Isa al Masih is the Word of God. He has the authority to command things, and they happen. Isa is the Son of God because he is the Word of God, and because he does the will of his Father. God was always with Isa where ever he was going, because he came from God and was following his words. God cannot father a child like humans; he simply commands things and they happen – that's what happened in the birth of Isa al Masih."

The bystander, looking a bit disturbed by what he was hearing, spoke up again, "If we believe what you say, should we no longer go for prayers?"

"My fellow Muslims, God brought the message of salvation through Abraham. He had two sons, and God told Abraham that he would bless all people and tribes through them. The other nations needed someone to correct them. If we don't understand, we will go astray. Correction has come to us. That correction is that all the nations will be blessed through Abraham.

"So if we want to follow God, we need to make sure we understand the promise to Abraham. What did the followers of Isa say, and what did the followers of Muhammad say? These two, Isa and Muhammad, were not confused. But if it is confusing, it is we who are confused about what God wants. Because what we want is not like what God wants.

Musa, his voice increasing in strength and volume, continued, "Check many religions. Their father is Abraham. Abraham was in a good relationship with God, and God gave him many children so that people should follow Abraham as an example."

Becoming mildly confrontational, he finished saying, "Each person should think about his own life!"

Someone else in the group asked, "Why do you speak so much of Isa al Masih?"

Musa answered, "The testimony Isa gave is completely true. For example, what Isa said about the signs of the end time is true. I believe the messiah will return. Even the Quran says so. The messiah ascended to heaven just as he said he would, and he will come back."

Speaking with a strength that belied his age and frailty, Musa asked, "Didn't he say so before the Quran came? After he said this, the Quran came, and said Isa al Masih was the Word of God. This means that the Son of God is not a liar."

"So do you believe that Isa al Masih died on a cross?" The stranger spoke up again, but his voice had lost its accusing tone.

Musa answered, "We can believe the testimony of Isa's death, because he foretold it before death came to him. He said, 'One of you will betray me.' And he also predicted, 'The Son of God will see terrible sufferings through one of you.' So we believe what he said, because this is what happened. And everyone saw it; it happened in the open. Isa also predicted, 'After I die, I will be three days in the grave, but I will rise again and show myself so that you will believe that what I'm saying is completely true.' And it happened just as he said it would. He was in the grave for three days, then he rose again and lived. After that, many people saw him and spoke to him. This proves that what he said was true. He does not tell lies."

Musa, clearly tired by now, carried on in a fainter voice, "All these things give proof to a person like me. Everything he predicted happened as he said it would. Because of this, my heart has believed that Isa doesn't tell a lie. That's it. That is what I have to say. For those who believe, it will be a blessing. For those who do not believe, it will be their misfortune. If I have made a mistake, please correct me. Peace be upon you all."

Later, Musa sat with Paul in the shade of his porch. "I have to tell you something. Fourteen years ago, I had collected sap from a tree to make a bird trap. I hid and watched a large bird come and land in my sap. I thought it was stuck, so I jumped up to catch it. But as I came close, I was surprised to see that it was not a bird after all. It was a person! A man in bright white! He told me, 'What you long for will be fulfilled after fourteen years.' I went home puzzling over this strange occurrence. Fourteen years later, I met you. When we were talking about Isa al Masih, I remembered that this was what I wanted. This was the fulfilment of what that shining man told me fourteen years ago.

"My whole life, I have been like a prisoner let out on bail, just waiting for the judgement day and the punishment I deserve. With this hanging over me, I was not really free. Now, since I have received forgiveness through Isa al Masih, I am free. I no longer fear punishment; I no longer fear death."

Epilogue

As he sat in the shade of his porch, Shaykh Musa shared with his neighbours his current understanding of Bible passages such as Genesis 16, John 1 and 5, Romans 4, and Matthew 24. While his theology may not be perfect, it provides an example of a theology in process. It's a messy process when people go through a change of worldview – from one shaped by other beliefs and fears, to one shaped by Biblical truth and the Spirit of God. Today, Musa continues to allow the Bible to shift his cultural biases. This process, which took centuries in the West, is helping Musa and others like him to build a culturally relevant identity as a follower of Isa without compromising the gospel, which helps others in their culture consider following him also.

Eric Adams and his wife Laura pioneered an effort to take the good news to Muslims in South Asia. They now live in England.

Stoking the Home Fire

by Clare Janzen

Equipped with faith, youth, and an impossible dream, Jack and Barb moved to Eastern Europe 25 years ago. Their belief in the power of the living God motivated their decision, but the nominally Muslim, officially atheistic nation that occupied their prayers didn't issue visas to foreigners. So they moved to a neighbourhood with a majority of the people they hoped to reach in a city across the border and began to adapt to the culture. As they became fluent in the language, their integration with this community forged an identity that re-defined their future.

A cruel dictatorship that allowed little freedom of thought had crushed all religious affiliations over the past half century. Even so, family identities were tied to Muslim or orthodox Christian backgrounds, and community values reflected centuries of tradition – both inside the nation and in these displaced refugee groups.

When a sudden change of government opened the borders, Jack and Barb's dream became reality almost-instantly. Within weeks, they had moved into the capital city, where oppression had left its ugly scar. In its collapsed economy, only a few basic food items were available. The impoverished people were hungry for anything brought in from the West. Food rations and meaningful conversations were both equally welcome. The collapse of political structures allowed a flood of aid and aid workers to engage the nation. The former tyrannical opposition had vanished, but no religious groups or faithful worshipers had survived the long reign of terror.

Hassan, a teenager at the time, had trained for a career as a folk musician playing the accordion. Like many others, he made an illegal dash through the borders as soon as they opened, in pursuit of a better life. When his unmet dreams crashed around him, he cried out for help to a God he didn't even believe in. Within days, he was repatriated by authorities.

Home again, wandering grey streets that echoed with familiar despair, he noticed a group meeting on the steps of the city stadium. Curiosity trumped misery, and he moved closer to hear a message of hope – healing and freedom through Jesus the Messiah. The promise of Light began to invade the shadows over his heart. Hassan and Jack met that day.

Soon, Hassan was spending hours in Jack's home, drinking tea and deliberating the ideas introduced at weekly meetings. These discussions opened new doors in the tight world of ideas and values that Hassan had known. Until now, government, culture, and school curriculum had hemmed his world with tall walls, no doors, and few windows.

Jack's questions prompted discoveries that represented the freedom that had evaded him during his aborted flight to the West.

Photo credit: iStockPhoto

Hassan's school teachers had always been cruel and demeaning. Jack asked probing questions with genial persistence. When Jack's words were sharp, he was quick to restore the relationship with a sincere apology. In Hassan's family, harsh words of conflict were an unrelenting requiem; he didn't know the music of harmony and resolution. Watching Jack and Barb and their family, Hassan began to dream that someday his own family relationships would reflect their gentle principles of grace and compassion.

Hassan's dreams cultivated understanding, which gave birth to faith and with it a commitment to follow the ways of Jesus. He joined a small group that studied the life and teachings of the Messiah. Soon, Hassan was leading this group, using the Bible and some simple questions that Jack wrote. The questions required honest responses about relationships, personal thoughts, and behaviour. Robust discussions, like a well-fuelled fire, lasted long into the night.

Hassan, who had never led a group or taught a class in his life, was on a learning curve. As he watched Jack, who dealt with his own shortcomings with transparency, Hassan became honest about his own struggles. It felt easy to ask for help when the responsibility was too much – Jack deliberately created that opportunity and need.

Hassan was soon part of a second group made up of leaders of other small groups. Jack recognized in these young men the leadership qualities of faithfulness and initiative. Most importantly, he chose as leaders those who were dealing appropriately with areas of weakness and sin. He connected with them at a heart level and tried to model the character he hoped they would achieve. By living openly, talking about his own struggles, shortcomings, and temptations and asking for their prayers, Jack developed friendships that engendered genuine trust and maturity. As they grew, the young leaders took on more responsibility for others.

Within the small groups, each member made a covenant with one other person. They committed to grow together as followers of Jesus. Discipline in daily prayer for each other and a weekly review of life issues created friendships that laid a foundation in ministry for years to come.

Hassan and others in the leadership group began lobbying Jack to purchase a building for meetings. They saw benefits in such a purchase, but Jack could not agree. They argued that the identity of the young community of faith would benefit from a western-style building in which to hold public meetings, explaining that family, neighbours, and friends respected a religious group based on its size and constancy.

These discussions, while controversial, indicated that the young leaders were taking ownership of the growth process. Like a fire that has burst with flaming kindling, then settles into the steady glow of matured wood, the heated dialogue indicated progress.

Their society viewed small groups meeting in homes as untrustworthy, a passing phenomenon, or worse – a cult. Eventually, Jack agreed, conceding that a public meeting with people from many educational backgrounds and all levels of society attending would add to the authenticity and respectability of the growing group. They couldn't buy a building, but they rented an old puppet theatre.

Still, the larger meetings challenged Jack's ideals. Knowing that the best character growth develops in small accountable groups, he thought the larger meetings took unnecessary energy and effort. He could see how popular they were and how they generated a critical mass of attendees, keeping things stable when some of the youthful leaders went out to start groups in smaller cities. In fact, when the larger meetings were suspended, the smaller meetings seemed to shrink in size.

Love for western music also wove its way into the heart of these public meetings. Jack challenged this trend. He suggested they should have music that reflected the local culture, but they argued that this reminded them of their years of oppression, saying, "We want songs that fill us with hope." He reluctantly conceded this point as well.

In meetings held in the puppet theatre, Jack pushed the young leaders forward to teach and lead worship while he stayed in the background. He wanted to ensure that the meetings were culturally appropriate, and he expected these young men would grow into the role. He was willing to let them spread their wings and fly, even if it meant he had to push them off a cliff. It didn't work as well as he had hoped, but his conviction that God planned to transform the nation fuelled his energy and balanced his concerns. Three years after the borders burst open, Jack handed the leadership of the fledgling church to the local elders. He was convinced that this was in keeping with the strategy of the apostle Paul.

Hassan and three other elders carried the vision as best they could, but the blaze of their early fervour quickly dimmed to glowing embers. Following Jack's example, these elders pushed others onto the platform, and the quality of teaching and worship waned.

They approached Jack, who was now coaching and training others around the country, and begged him to return to his role in their leadership team. When he refused, they came back, imploring him again, "We need you. Please, please help us. We need your leadership. Something is missing when you are not here."

Jack steadfastly refused their request, answering with a local proverb: "Only a native knows where the roof leaks." He acknowledged the struggle but felt the rocky beginning was inevitable. He remained convinced that when they found their footing, they would lead the group better than he ever could.

As the numbers slipped lower and momentum slowed across the years, Jack's optimism turned to alarm. The meetings were no longer a time of celebration. They had become a depressing statement of grim determination. Their joy in gathering together had lost its place to dogged faithfulness.

The leaders repeated their litany of requests, and Jack wrestled with his previous confidence. How could he go wrong in following Paul's method? He had discussed the situation at length, and he knew his wife, his mentor, and his organisation all agreed. Things would return to normal, and growth would surely resume – with a little more time.

But this optimism failed to carry him through the next year. Jack's doubts grew. After all, no one had proven this strategy, in this nation, under the weight of these social needs, during this time of upheaval. Jack felt the passion of his first vision and faith for this nation weren't dovetailing with what was happening. It wasn't just the group he had started that struggled to keep going; many others were in similar distress. With the fires of small fellowships turning cold throughout the nation, Jack began to cry out for answers.

On a summer retreat, Jack crept into a place of solitude. As he lifted his tormenting questions to God, they were replaced with a quiet, but potent message that brought tranquillity: "Just trust me." The answer was not to find the right strategy, the right leaders, or the right way forward. He knew he needed faith in the One whose glory covers the earth. As surely as air blankets this planet, the glory of God was covering this nation, and God was in control. Jack needed to keep his confidence fixed on God's presence, not his own strategy. Jack returned home in peace.

A few months passed. One early morning, in bracing winter weather, Jack tiptoed away from the home of a local leader he was visiting, while everyone still slept. Climbing a hill overlooking the quiet village, Jack felt the warmth of God's presence. With it came a growing conviction of what he should do next. It was not what he expected or wanted to hear, so at first he doubted that this was God's direction. But for three weeks he had not been able to shake the idea and on this morning, he was convinced enough to ask God to confirm it through the consent of both his wife and his mentor – something he would consider a near miracle.

On his arrival back from the frosty hill, Jack's host greeted him with a cup of tea – a cultural invitation to sit together. With none of the habitual polite morning greetings, this leader peered at Jack and with uncharacteristic bluntness told him, "The biggest mistake you've made since you came to this country was to give up the leadership of that first church. You should go back to leading it."

His words echoed the idea Jack had been grappling with before God. Although this might be confirmation, Jack knew the more important agreement must come from Barb. He wasted no time laying out his thoughts, sharing what he had been wrestling with, asking her advice. "Honey," he assured her, "If this is from the Lord, I believe you will think so, too. Please don't feel pressured to agree; just pray about it."

Doubtful that he would find agreement, Jack wrote his mentor, explaining the situation. "This is barely working, and it's certainly not flourishing. We've been going backward for several years, and if we don't do something now, our work could result in small, struggling fellowships with no real progress toward a national movement into God's kingdom. Furthermore, should I continue to try to reproduce something that isn't working in the first place? I don't want to light any more fires until I have the home fire burning strong."

The coach's reply stunned Jack. "Give it a try. See if, after a couple of years, this is the right way to go." Jack could barely believe what he was reading. Barb, equally surprised, continued to deliberate. Jack made a studied attempt not to pressure her. After considering it, she agreed to the coach's suggestion – it was worth a try.

Jack's return to leadership carried a bold conviction. "I made a switch in my heart: I took initiative openly and unapologetically, modelling the kind of leader I wanted locals to be. The leaders and elders needed to see what they wanted to reproduce. I had been a lamb hoping to give birth to lions."

In the public celebrations that Jack had previously seen as superfluous, he saw vision and energy come alive. The large meetings picked up momentum first, and then the small fellowships experienced renewed interest and a burst of growth. They named the small groups "Bible Families" and watched as relationships grew. With commitment to one another, the members did indeed sense that they were close, like families.

Jack, Hassan, and other leaders watched these changes and discussed why small fellowships had burned out all over the country. They wondered if it was related to the identity provided by the larger, public meeting that seemed to provide dynamic synergy. Perhaps the house-church strategy wasn't right for the social climate of a nation still struggling to find its feet. Or maybe it just wasn't God's plan for this time. They were grateful for the answer to their prayers and for the growth that would continue over the next decade.

Today, Hassan and other leaders occasionally meet over an Italian cappuccino in a trendy, downtown coffee house. The music is loud, the colours are splashy, and there is a play space for children, including Hassan's. Inside, nothing recalls the years of hunger and the legacy of an oppressed nation. Outside, on streets once occupied by decrepit, rusting public transport, traffic is congested with shiny family cars. There are still a few children in rags, but now they are the exception; for most, life is a scramble to catch up with the rest of the world.

Rented facilities still host the weekend meeting, now in an open space at the top of an office complex. Hassan arrives in a church owned VW Caddy that transports electronic keyboards, speakers, sound boards, and guitars to the building. This is his week to take leadership in getting everything set up. He begins the taxing effort of lugging it all up three flights of stairs.

The meeting will include widows, teenagers, government officials, wealthy businessmen, even beggars, all gathering together – accepted on equal footing. Everyone is welcome, and no one is exempt from a relationship of committed prayer and accountability as they become part of the community.

Jack now says, "My early expectations were unrealistically dependent on strategy I had learned in seminary in another culture. I learned the hard way not to apply strategy unless it has been tested for suitability to the situation. In this case, I was not factoring the importance of the mosque to the Muslim identity. Muslims here would never consider practising their faith without a mosque; it's part of their psyche. Mostly, I learned from my mistakes, and this was one of them. The heart is always more important than the form."

As the elders recall their early years together, a strong sense of agreement emerges. Small meetings, held during the week, are the essence of their faith community, but a large group event with its predictable schedule and visible presence provides credibility in the eyes of newcomers.

Hassan's wife explains, "This culture is not one that values personal uniqueness or individualism. To be 'other' is not a good thing. When you only have five or ten people meeting together, you are not credible. No one wants to be a part of that. Neighbours ask, 'How big is your group?' When they hear it is in the hundreds, they start to take it seriously and are willing to consider it. When you invite someone from your work or neighbourhood, this is one of the biggest factors that will influence their decision to come – or not."

Youth leader Ali agrees, "Just this last week, I visited a teenager and his family. He started coming, and then stopped. His family told him he couldn't attend anything religious. But when they heard that we have a public meeting with up to three hundred people attending, it made all the difference."

Abdyl, an elder who leads a village fellowship, says, "We all agree that the midweek meeting is the important one. That's where relationships are real, where we share our joys and sorrows, our fears, and our dreams. That's where scripture application takes place, and where we are really a church. However, the larger weekly gathering provides something else we need – something we can't survive without. I don't want to plant a big church like this out in the village. In that setting, the women won't even meet with the men. This kind of meeting wouldn't work. But I know this: Without this meeting here in town, with its worship and good sermons, I wouldn't have what I need to carry on. And I know the villagers expect to be able to come to some big meetings from time to time to refresh their faith in a manner they cannot find in the village."

Though he agrees that the small meeting is essential, Hakim adds – "This (gesturing at the large hall) is important, too. Here we know we will get great quality teaching. And sometimes it's necessary to have a place to just be silent before the Lord, with no one asking you questions." An accomplished musician, Hakim has begun to write worship songs with local rhythms and poetic themes that reflect the culture – just as Jack had originally hoped.

Hassan and Jack's friendship has spanned nearly two decades, having grown from a shy beginning to that of respected colleagues. The musician has traded his accordion for a guitar and keyboard – and his dreams of escaping to freedom for contentment ministering as a shepherd like David. As Hassan opens his vehicle and unloads the heavy equipment, Jack arrives, picks up the sound board and begins to climb the three flights of stairs.

Hassan summarises what he has learned from Jack with this observation, "Jack is available to the congregation every week. He's always here early to help carry things upstairs. He takes out the garbage without complaining, attending even menial chores. He has taught me something I never knew existed before I met him – that a leader can be a servant. That ideal doesn't even exist in my culture. It would never be considered. All the leaders I ever knew were dictators – until I met Jack."

The home fire is burning once again.

Clare Janzen is a wife and mother to a lively family of six (four siblings, two parents). She has lived in North Africa and waits for the fulfilment of the promise of Isaiah 35: "The desert shall rejoice and blossom as a rose."

Uncle, Is It True?

by Eric Adams

The young man walked down the dusty street of the market, looking self-conscious dressed in robes that mark him as from the countryside. He made his way through the throng of shoppers bartering with merchants, milling at the open booths and looking for bargains at the end of the day. Even now, some of the shopkeepers were striking the awnings, packing away their vegetables, meats, fabrics, and pots for tomorrow's business. He dodged between a man loaded down with plastic bags and a housewife in intense discussion with a greengrocer over carrots.

He finally saw the stall he was looking for, filled with cans and jars on the shelves, open drums of flour and maize, sacks of rice and millet, small plastic bags with nuts and crackers, large plastic bags of oil. The owner of the stall was beginning to bring in his wares and seal his goods to protect them from rats and other pests. Daud slowed and walked toward the man. "Peace be upon you," he said quietly. "Uncle Yusuf, how are you? I bring greetings from your brother, from your family."

The man turned, a broad smile on his face. "And upon you be peace, Daud!" he cried. "I am well. You are a pleasant sight for an old man, my son. Let me finish locking up, then let's go have tea and you can tell me about the family."

The storekeeper closed the doors to his shop and secured them for the night. They then walked together through the rubbish-filled streets and entered the courtyard that Daud's uncle shared with several other families. In one corner, boys were playing with a wheel and stick. In another was a sheep pen made of bits of old wood and rusty tin roofing. They went into one of the rooms, sparsely furnished, with paint peeling off the walls. Daud greeted his aunt. Once they had settled on the mats on the floor, Yusuf quietly asked his wife to bring tea and dinner.

Daud ate hungrily. He had travelled far that day in the heat of the sun, on the back of an old pickup truck. As he ate, he told his uncle news of his family and village. Yusuf, whilst preparing glasses of hot, sweet tea, quietly listened and asked a few questions, exclaiming at the births and marriages, and growing sad at the announcements of the deaths of a few people he knew. The conversation slowed. Daud finished his rice and fish, then slurped his tea noisily. Yusuf smiled and encouraged Daud to say what was really on his mind. "You have not come all this way, my son, to tell me news about the family. What do you want to ask me? What is on your heart?"

"You are right, as usual, uncle." The young man hesitated, then began, "It's Hassan, uncle. You know his story?"

The older man nodded and said, "Yes. Your cousin, the one delivered from the spirits."

"Yes, uncle," the young man continued, "I saw it happen. I came with Hassan to the city here. I was with him and the foreigners who talked about the Prophet Isa. At the time, Hassan couldn't eat or drink. He would just stay in the corner and stare off into space. I had thought it was those foreigners who had done this to him. I had also gone to the meetings where they told stories about the prophets Adam, Moses, David, and Isa. At first, Hassan was very excited by these stories. But then, as the days went on, he withdrew into himself and became closed to the world. He became like one asleep with his eyes open."

Yusuf nodded and Daud continued, "We brought him to the house where the foreigners prayed over Hassan for days, and nothing seemed to happen. They asked me if they could take off his protective fetishes and destroy them. I was afraid; this was a serious thing. I thought maybe they were the only thing still protecting Hassan. Finally, I said they could take them off, but I did not have the authority to allow them to destroy them. After all, they're expensive! They put Hassan on a water drip into his arm so he wouldn't die for lack of water. Then they prayed even more for another week. They took Hassan to the hospital where they gave him some medicine, but he just got worse and worse.

"Uncle, I was afraid. Hassan's brother Hamid had come to see him. Did you know he is a follower of Isa? Hamid gave permission to destroy the fetishes. He went to the beach with Adam, one of the foreigners, and they destroyed them together. I waited at the hospital with Hassan.

"While they were away, Hassan suddenly began to drink again. Later that night, we took him back to the house, and he improved rapidly over the next two days. One night the foreigners came to the house and they were praising God together. Suddenly Hassan sat up and was praising him as well! I was so excited!

"Later, Hassan told us what was happening in his soul. He said, 'I was aware that whole time of what was going on. I was in the world where spirits go after death. I was watching a battle going on between you foreigners and the evil powers.'

Photo credit: Matt Brandon, www.thedigitaltrekker.com

This was how he described it, uncle. He said, 'I could see the battle going on. And I could see that when you foreigners were praying, you were winning the battle. But when you stopped, darkness would close in again. It was a huge fight, and I couldn't do anything about it.'

"And then Hassan said, 'In the hospital, all of a sudden, I suddenly felt this thing come out of my mouth. It was just like this presence came out of me, and I was able to drink again.' Later on, as Adam and the other foreigners talked, we realized this was the moment Hamid and Adam destroyed the fetish on the beach.

"Hassan told us, 'This thing or presence was blocking my throat. That was the reason I couldn't swallow or speak, because it was strangling me. It was choking me. When they destroyed the fetish, I was free. And when you brought me back in the house and you were worshiping God, I was filled with his presence. It was an absolute joy. I had to sit up and join in!'"

Daud's eyes had gotten a bit moist as he recounted this dramatic episode to his uncle. He blinked and looked down as he took another sip of his tea.

"And how is Hassan now? Yusuf asked.

"You know, uncle," Daud replied, "most of the time he is well, and his heart is light. But sometimes, when he is tempted to go back to magic and fetishes, you can see the fight for his soul in his eyes. He becomes quiet, as if he is no longer present. The foreigners have told me that they pray regularly for him, and for all of us."

Daud finished. The uncle and nephew sat silent for a few moments.

"So, my son, what do you want to ask me?"

The young man looked at him for a moment, then said, "Uncle, why do you follow the Prophet Isa?"

Yusuf sat back in his chair and smiled. "That's an excellent question, my son!"

"It started many years ago. I remember when the first foreigners arrived. Like many people in town, I had heard lots of stories about the one man called Sulayman. (In his language, he is called Hans.) One day he was in front of the mosque after Friday prayers. A group had gathered around him, shouting abuse. They say he was almost stoned right there on the street. However, he just answered them quietly, in beautiful Arabic, and eventually walked away unharmed.

"This incident made me intensely curious about these infidels. I found out that instead of living in a big house like wealthy people, Sulayman, his family, and his colleagues lived among the poorest people in our city. They helped poor people by providing food for widows and children. They were sacrificing themselves for our sakes. At the time, I thought to myself, 'We should be doing that, that's what the Quran tells us to do!' I realized that we are content just to throw a few small pieces of money to beggars on the street. They, the infidels, shamed us by the actions of their lives.

"I knew they were followers of the Prophet Isa, and I began noticing the stories about him in the Quran. I had been impressed with the greatness of Isa al Masih. I wanted to know more about him.

"Eventually I was able to meet the foreigner Adam. He told me more stories about Isa. They impressed me, but I had to know whether the beliefs of the foreign followers of the Prophet Isa were genuine, so I began testing them. I would ask Adam questions about the Quran and about their books. He spoke our language well. He was knowledgeable and gracious. More importantly, his life was consistent with his words. It amazed me. Over time, I began to ask why he was like this. He told me stories about the prophets and about Isa al Masih. The more I learned, the more my heart wanted to follow Isa. Eventually, I surrendered my life to Isa al Masih."

Daud sat, absorbing the details for a minute. "Uncle, was this when you destroyed the iron shirt? Everybody in the family has talked about you and that iron shirt."

The older man nodded, "Yes. Your aunt was very angry at the time. That shirt was worth a lot of money. I didn't tell her what I was doing, but she knew when I had destroyed it. Though she wasn't with us when we destroyed it in the desert, she felt it somehow, and she was shaking with fear at the time. She almost asked for a divorce from me because of what I'd done."

Daud looked puzzled. "Why did you destroy something that was so powerful? I heard it could stop bullets! Your grandfather's grandfather passed it down to you, right?"

Yusuf smiled at his nephew. "My son, I had to destroy it for the same reason that they had to destroy Hassan's fetishes. These things have power that comes from evil jinn, not from God. This kind of power might give us short-term benefit, but ultimately it imprisons and destroys our hearts with fear. I couldn't go on following Isa al Masih if I let this shirt exist. Others told me it was impossible to destroy that shirt. But Adam and I took it into the desert and prayed to break the power of the jinn over it. Then it burned easily."

"How did you break the power of those jinn?" Daud asked.

"It was through the greater authority that Isa al Masih gives all his followers. Adam and I prayed together and broke the spell. The Prophet Isa is far more powerful than an iron shirt. To keep the shirt would have meant that I didn't fully trust the power of the Word of God. Isa al Masih wants us to surrender to God with our whole heart, soul, mind, and strength. To give allegiance to him only as king so I can be a subject of his kingdom."

Daud thought about this for a few minutes, then said, "Uncle, is it true that they put you in prison for following the Prophet Isa?"

"Yes, that's also true. But only for a few days. And many of our tribe's leaders came to comfort your aunt. They told her, 'We know why your husband's in prison. We don't agree with him, but we respect him so much that we're here to support you. We'll do everything we can to get him released.'

"And they did help me gain my freedom. When I was released, they told me, 'We don't agree with your faith, but we stand with you because you are a man of honour and integrity who blesses your community through the work you do.'"

"Is that because of the school you run for poor children, uncle?"

"Yes. That and other things. We keep high standards for the school, so lots of families send their children. And we take them – whether or not they can pay. We trust that God will provide what we need to run the school. And God does provide."

At that moment, they heard a man's voice from the door: "Peace be upon you!"

Yusuf's eyes lit up. "And upon you be peace!" he responded, standing as they greeted one another. Turning, Yusuf said,

"This is my brother's son, Daud, from my village. Son, this is my friend Ibrahim." Daud and Ibrahim politely exchanged greetings, news, and inquiries about each other's health.

Ibrahim sat with them, accepting tea from Yusuf's wife. Yusuf gave his friend a searching look and said, "And how is the health of your family? Your wife and child are well?"

Ibrahim's eyes gleamed, "She is well, praise God, and the child is well. God is blessing our family."

Yusuf smiled, "So God is giving you a new one!"

Ibrahim nodded and said quietly, "Yes, she is with child again."

Yusuf sat back. "Praise God!"

Turning to Daud, Ibrahim said, "Have you heard the story of God's gift to my family?"

Daud tutted a soft click with his tongue to indicate "no."

Ibrahim told his story with a smile on his face. "My wife couldn't conceive. We had waited for a child for many years. We were so ashamed and had spent all our money buying charms from the spiritual leaders and healers. Finally, in desperation, we went to the foreigners three years ago, and we prayed together for her. She conceived a few weeks later, and now we have our daughter. We call her Hiba – gift of God. Praise be to God!"

Yusuf smiled and asked, "Where have you come from, friend?"

"I just came from a village up north near the river. A spiritual leader in that village had had a dream about the Prophet

Isa and wanted to know more about him. When I arrived, another follower of Isa from a nearby village was already there. God is raising up so many followers of Isa across the country!

"I stayed there for a few days. The brother and I together told stories of Adam and Eve, the prophets, and Isa al Masih. As we told the stories, the spiritual leader would repeat them, and the villagers would listen because he affirmed the stories with his authority. Now there is a group in that village who are learning to follow Isa. I left a copy of the Torah and the Injil with the leader, who can read. I will visit again in a month or two and see how they are coming along."

"Praise God!" said Yusuf. "Last week one of the foreigners and I took the film about the Prophet Isa to a village where we heard there was a believer. We began setting up a projector and large screen in his compound. As darkness descended, people began to show up and sit on the ground. By the time we began to show the film, there were several hundred in his courtyard. They were sitting so close they couldn't move! Half the village must have been there."

"Yes," Ibrahim said, "I've seen the same thing happen. People will come because they want to hear a film in their own language. But the story of the Prophet Isa grips their hearts."

"We used a truck battery to run the projector," Yusuf continued. "Half way through the film, the battery gave out and the people left, disappointed that they hadn't seen the end. There was no electricity in the village, of course. Only one person in the village had a solar panel – the leader at the mosque. He was a relative of the follower of Isa, so we went to ask him whether he would recharge the battery. When we had explained the situation, the imam said, 'Yes, you can charge the battery, no problem. However, I want to see the film as well.'

"So the next day, after the battery was charged, we took the equipment to the imam's big house. He and 20 of his disciples watched it that afternoon. They were riveted by it. We stopped in the middle so they could perform their afternoon prayers. Then we continued to the end, including the part about surrendering our life to Isa al Masih. They were very touched by it and asked many questions.

"That night, more people turned up, so we showed the film to maybe 500 people. We had to start from the beginning again. They are interested in The Prophet Isa. Some people in the village will keep on telling the stories of the prophets and of Isa al Masih. I will travel there again in a few months to see what God is doing. We pray he will establish a gathering of believers in Isa al Masih."

"Praise God!" said Ibrahim, smiling. "This is well done."

The three sipped fresh cups of tea in silence for a few moments, then Daud asked, "Uncles, you follow the Prophet Isa. But is this way a foreign thing? You talk a lot about the foreigners. Are they running this?"

Ibrahim and Yusuf exchanged a knowing look. "That is an insightful question, my son," said Yusuf. "It is true that foreigners brought knowledge of the power and truth of Isa al Masih to us. They lived with the character of The Prophet Isa among us. They served us, learned our tongue, suffered, and sacrificed as they learned to tell us this message."

He remembered an evening 12 years ago when the foreigners invited people who wanted to follow Isa al Masih to meet together. No one wanted to come, because they were strangers to each other. "It was a struggle for us as believers because we didn't know each other. This group met in the houses of the foreigners. There was no trust amongst us, and some followed Isa for personal gain. They thought they would get money. They thought the foreigners would help them escape abroad. This group did not hold together. It melted away.

"More recently, the foreigners encouraged some believers to go to their families and demonstrate the changed heart The Prophet Isa has given them, and as they gained respect and a hearing, to share this hope within them with family and friends. Eventually, family and friends listened. They were often convinced by seeing their changed hearts. This good news about Isa al Masih has begun to spread now from family to family, village to village. There are many we don't know about. We just hear rumours that others are now following Isa al Masih. It is a new thing God is doing. Praise God."

Ibrahim agreed, "It is true, my son, that we looked to the foreigners as teachers at first. They taught us much wisdom that obviously comes from God. Recently, however, they encouraged us to make more of the decisions together. We are adjusting to this. It was a lot easier when they made these decisions. But they continue to look to us, who must then look to God, before we act."

Yusuf said, "The leaders of the many gatherings are now meeting together and becoming more comfortable thinking about decisions. We still work closely with the foreigners, but now we decide together. We are learning."

Ibrahim considered what would happen if the Islamists force the foreigners from the country, as they would like to do. "We will need to stand on our own, by the will of God," he thought. He knew that gatherings of Isa followers were increasing throughout the country. He had even heard of some across the borders and among other tribes in the north.

Speaking aloud, he said to Daud, "This seems to be a work of God among our people, but I wonder how it will end. The foreigners are helping us through training and encouraging us not to become dependent on them for money, to set up businesses and other ways to support this ministry God has given us. One day they will leave. This will be hard."

Daud nodded, thoughtfully. "Uncle, what happens in these meetings? What do people who are followers of Isa do?"

"It is very simple, my son," said Yusuf, "as families watch their herds or move them to new grazing grounds, the followers of Isa naturally gather together for teaching, prayer, breaking bread for the memory of Isa and fellowship together. This is something that's known in the Injil."

Surprised, Daud said, "This is something we can easily do in our village!"

Ibrahim smiled, "Yes, and when we do it under the lordship of Isa al Masih, our hearts sing."

Daud looked thoughtful. "Uncle, could I come and join in with this group, take part in these things, and learn more about The Prophet Isa?"

Yusuf smiled, "Of course, my son. I will travel to the village with you and we will break bread with our family together in the name of Isa al Masih. Many others in the village often join us, both believers and seekers. We can study together what it says about these things in the Injil."

Eric Adams pioneered an effort to take the good news to Muslims in South Asia. He now resides in England.

About the Stories

If you live among Muslims and invite them to follow Jesus with you - or if you hope to in the future - the rest of this book provides you with information and tools to help you reflect on that great work of the gospel. First is an explanation about the sources of these stories.

What are Fruitful Practice Stories?

"Great are the works of the LORD; they are pondered by all who delight in them" (Psalm 111:2).

The stories in this volume were intended to help readers study and ponder the "works of the LORD" among Muslims today. The Fruitful Practices Narratives Project was commissioned to produce case studies that illustrate key fruitful practices. In this context, "fruitful practices" refer to activities that promote the emergence, vitality, and multiplication of fellowships of Jesus followers in a Muslim context. The Fruitful Practices List (presented in the next section) is the result of a multi-year, multi-agency study conducted by Fruitful Practice Research. This list of 68 practices includes short descriptions of practices that, through research, have been correlated with "fruitful" efforts.

For more information about the background and source of these fruitful practices and for a more complete explanation of each of the practices, see *From Seed to Fruit: Global Trends, Fruitful Practices, and Emerging Issues among Muslims* (J. Dudley Woodberry, ed. Pasadena, CA: William Carey Library, 2008).

Who has Conducted this Study?

Fruitful Practice Research is a multi-agency team who conduct primary research, analyse the research, create tools to help field teams benefit from the research, develop materials to train field teams in reflective practice, and produce materials to make the research accessible to others. We view the study of fruitful practices through the wider lens of knowledge stewardship.

For the most recent updates on this research and tools to help you use it, visit www.fruitfulpractice.org. Fruitful Practice Research serves a network of international agencies, and content on the website is for members only. Partner agencies arrange access for their members. If you need help to access this site, please write to *info@fruitfulpractice.org*.

Using the Stories

Because these stories are from real life, none of them provide perfect examples of fruitful practices at work. Real life is messier than that. Many of the principles practiced helped to bear fruit, some less so. The stories, with their successes and challenges, provide examples that can help you reflect on your own work.

In this section are two tools designed to help you reflect on and learn from the stories you've read. You'll find group discussion guides for each story. The guides are followed by the complete list of fruitful practices – not all of which have been illustrated within the stories in this book. The list includes some questions for reflection that you may use alone or with a team.

Discussion Guides

How to Use the Discussion Guides

The purpose of these guides is to help a leader conduct a discussion with a group of people who have already read one of the narratives. Discussion groups should probably be no more than 10-12 people. Here are some things to do to prepare before you lead a discussion:

- Provide a copy of the story to each person who will participate in the discussion. Ask everyone to read it before the date you set for your discussion.

- If you haven't done so already, make yourself familiar with the Fruitful Practices List on page 148. Each guide provides a list of practices that were illustrated in the story. Be ready to highlight those at appropriate points in the discussion.

- As the leader, read the questions and think about your own answers to all of the discussion questions.

- Read through the questions and think about how you will conduct the discussion. Plan for ways to give everyone a chance to contribute. The most important thing is to get your group to reflect on your own practices and think together about any changes you may want to make.

Discussion: Not a Foreign Message

To prepare beforehand, the leader should follow the steps outlined on page 117.

Some fruitful practices you may note in this story

As a leader, be ready to highlight the following practices during the discussion. Research has shown these practices to be correlated with fruitfulness across a wide variety of ministry situations among Muslims.

- **Seekers 5**: Fruitful workers begin discipling seekers as part of the process of coming to faith.

- **Seekers 6**: Fruitful workers encourage seekers to share what God is doing in their lives.

- **Believers 1**: Fruitful workers are intentional in their discipling.

- **Believers 2**: Fruitful workers disciple in locally appropriate and reproducible ways.

- **Believers 5**: Fruitful workers help believers find ways to remain within their social network.

- **Believers 9**: Fruitful workers encourage believers to share their faith.

- **Leaders 2**: Fruitful leaders mentor leaders who in turn mentor others.

- **Communication 2**: Fruitful workers communicate the gospel using the heart language, except in situations where it is not appropriate.

- **Communication 6**: Fruitful workers use Bible study as a means of sharing the gospel.

Observe and consider

- **Question**: What stood out most to you in this story? How did this story make you feel? What did it make you think about?

- **Question**: When and how did Nabil's process of becoming a disciple of Isa al Masih begin?

  Possible answers include: His colleagues Pete and Dave started talking with him about God and the prophets and about their respective holy books.

- **Question**: What examples are there in this story of the gospel spreading through Nabil and Sami's social networks?

  Possible answers include: Nabil was beginning to share his faith with his family members. His colleagues at work were also interested in his encounter with Jesus. When his close friend Sami became a follower of Jesus, they invited their circle of friends to look at God's word together.

- **Question**: How did Nabil and Sami adapt the way they went about sharing the message of Christ with different groups of people in their environment?

  Possible answers include: With colleagues at work, Nabil is very outspoken as they talk about Jesus. Sami is outspoken with his immediate family, but is taking it more slowly within his wider clan. Nabil's sister, mother, and nephew are hearing him read from the Psalms and tell stories of the Messiah. Sami reads to his wife from the Injil and plays Biblical stories on cassette tape in his car.

- **Question**: Based on Nabil's story, what are some of the potential advantages and disadvantages of cross-cultural workers ministering in a trade language (such as English) rather than the local language?

    Advantages: Sharing your faith in a trade language can provide a quick start. Some people may think of English (or another trade language) as being prestigious.

    Disadvantages: Your friends might not know how to transfer what they learned in English into their own language for personal spiritual growth and study or for sharing with family and friends.

- **Question**: What are some of the advantages and disadvantages of local followers of Christ ministering in a trade language (such as English) rather than their own language?

    Possible answers include: Not everyone knows trade languages like English, so if people don't have scripture in their own language, they might not really understand when the scripture is being read. So the potential spread of the good news is limited. People might think the message is only for those who know English or who want to act in foreign ways. They may not see that the good news is for them as well.

- **Question**: Some readers have been surprised that Nabil is so open about having a Bible study with other young men. What factors in Nabil's situation might have made it easier to share with his friends?

    Possible answers include: They were people within his social network; they were people of equal status as him, rather than higher or lower status; they gathered in a manner and place that are normal for friends to get together in their culture.

Make it personal

For the exercise to be beneficial to your group, you will need to see whether you can apply any of the fruitful practices to your own situation. Here are some questions to help your group make it personal.

- What do you find challenging in this story?
- How can you help encourage the spread of the gospel within social networks?
- In your situation, is use of a trade language or foreign language instead of the heart language impeding the spread of the gospel?

Discussion: Couscous on Sunday

To prepare beforehand, the leader should follow the steps outlined on page 117.

Some fruitful practices you may note in this story

As a leader, be ready to highlight the following practices during the discussion. Research has shown these practices to be correlated with fruitfulness across a wide variety of ministry situations among Muslims.

Note: In this story, we can view the parents as "fruitful workers" among their children as well as members of their faith community.

- **Believers 10**: Fruitful workers prepare believers to explain why they believe.
- **Faith Communities 1**: Fruitful faith communities use the Bible as the central source for life, growth and mission.
- **Faith Communities 7**: Fruitful faith communities share meals and practice hospitality.
- **Faith Communities 11**: Fruitful faith communities involve their children in worship and ministry.
- **Faith Communities 15**: Fruitful faith communities generally meet in homes or other informal settings.

Observe and consider

- **Question**: What stood out most to you in this story? How did this story make you feel? What did it make you think about?

- **Question**: How does the young girl learn her faith? How does she practice her faith?

  Possible answers include: She learned from observing her parents. Her father helped her see that they were different and that was a good thing. He explained why their family don't need to sacrifice a lamb. She understands from her family that following Jesus is the only thing that matters in life.

- **Question**: Describe the relationships of the family members with their neighbours and colleagues.

  Possible answers include: Father has the respect of his work colleagues, and gains the respect of the head teacher. Children faced bullying at school, from both children and teachers. Mother clearly has friends among the neighbours, and the family gain a reputation for hospitality, even for difficult nieces.

- **Question**: In what ways do the members of the family live according to the local culture? In what ways do they live differently than the local culture?

  Possible answers include: They don't celebrate the feast of the sacrifice and do celebrate Christmas. They mark Sunday as their special day instead of Friday. But they don't do all the things her friends accuse her of doing (eating pork, worshipping three gods, or practicing immorality). The father shows respect to the head teacher, enough that they become friends in spite of their different faiths. The parents' marriage stands out as different from those of neighbours.

- **Question**: What evidence do you see of bold faith? What evidence do you see of persevering faith?

  Possible answers include: The father has been in prison before, and the police have come to talk to him "many times," yet he continues to practice his faith by attending a public church service with other Muslim background believers. The brothers both stood up for their faith in their classroom. Their father apologised that they did not behave correctly, but he was clear not to apologise for their beliefs. Their father is known as a man who loves to speak about the things of God. Their mother shows persevering faith in prayer when Father is taken by the police overnight.

- **Question**: What emphasis do the members of this family place on scripture? What emphasis do they place on developing relationship with God?

  In your discussion, help the group pay attention to the way that the family structure their family worship service after the public church service has been disrupted by the police and the way the children read the Bible and pray in the mornings.

- **Question**: Describe the relationships between the family and other believers.

  Possible answers include: They met in public worship at a church for a while; later, they invited others to join them for worship in their home. They shared meals together.

Make it personal

For the exercise to be beneficial to your group, you will need to see whether you can apply any of the fruitful practices to your own situation. Here are some questions to help your group make it personal.

- What do you find challenging in this story?
- What should guide decisions about the ways in which Jesus' followers embrace or reject local culture?
- In what ways is this family an example to you?
- What have you learned from this story that could encourage new followers of Jesus to live out their faith in their community?

Discussion: Meeting the Saviour through the Quran

To prepare beforehand, the leader should follow the steps outlined on page 117.

Some fruitful practices you may note in this story

As a leader, be ready to highlight the following practices during the discussion. Research has shown these practices to be correlated with fruitfulness across a wide variety of ministry situations among Muslims.

- **Society 6**: Fruitful workers take advantage of pre-field and on-field research to shape their ministry.

- **Seekers 1**: Fruitful workers are bold in witness.

- **Seekers 2**: Fruitful workers pray for God's supernatural intervention as a sign that confirms the gospel.

- **Seekers 5**: Fruitful workers begin discipling seekers as part of the process of coming to faith.

- **Communication 1**: Fruitful workers use culturally appropriate Bible passages to communicate God's message.

- **Communication 6**: Fruitful workers use Bible study as a means of sharing the gospel.

- **Communication 8**: Fruitful workers use the Quran as a bridge to sharing the biblical gospel.

Observe and consider

- **Question:** What stood out most to you in this story? How did this story make you feel? What did it make you think about?

- **Question:** How does Abu Roo establish his identity when he first arrives in his new country? What kind of reputation does he have among his students?

  Possible answers include: He lived his spiritual life openly in front of his students from the first day. He answered honestly, using terms they understood. He took a humble approach as a fellow follower of God, offering something of what he had experienced, but willing to listen to them, too. He also allowed people into his life closely enough that they could see his moral behaviour.

- **Question:** How does he end up studying the Bible with four Muslim guests?

  In your discussion, help the group pay attention to the way that Abu Roo invited people into dialog about spiritual matters as "people who are serious about our relationship with God." He invited them to study something they had never noticed in the Quran and look for further revelation in the Bible.

- **Question:** How is his approach to holy books different from what the seekers had previously experienced?

  Possible answers include: Abu Roo encourages seekers to understand the Injil by asking simple questions to clarify meaning.

- **Question:** The author says Abu Roo and his team concentrate on discipleship rather than conversion. What does that mean? How do they do that?

  Possible answers include: They don't seek "a decision," but rather they keep revealing the life and principles of Jesus to seekers. They trust God's spirit to bring truth alive through his word. Rather than seeking to convince seekers, they encourage seekers to ask God to reveal truth.

Make it personal

For the exercise to be beneficial to your group, you will need to see whether you can apply any of the fruitful practices to your own situation. Here are some questions to help your group make it personal.

- What do you find challenging in this narrative?
- What might you want to do differently?
- What might it look like for you to focus on discipling seekers even before they fully believe in Jesus? What changes in attitude might that require?

Discussion: Desperate Enough to Pray

To prepare beforehand, the leader should follow the steps outlined on page 117.

Some fruitful practices you may note in this story

As a leader, be ready to highlight the following practices during the discussion. Research has shown these practices to be correlated with fruitfulness across a wide variety of ministry situations among Muslims.

- **Society 4**: Fruitful workers mobilize extensive, intentional, and focused prayer.

- **Society 6**: Fruitful workers take advantage of pre-field and on-field research to shape their ministry.

- **Seekers 2**: Fruitful workers pray for God's supernatural intervention as a sign that confirms the gospel.

- **Seekers 3**: Fruitful workers pray for the needs of their friends in their presence.

- **God 1**: Fruitful workers practice an intimate walk with God.

- **God 2**: Fruitful workers engage in regular, frequent prayer.

- **God 3**: Fruitful workers persevere through difficulty and suffering.

- **Faith Communities 4**: Fruitful faith communities value networking together.

Observe and consider

- **Question:** What stood out most to you in this story? How did this story make you feel? What did it make you think about?

- **Question:** At whose initiative did the Campbells begin to focus on prayer?

  Consider this: The Campbells say the initiative for prayer seemed to be God's, not theirs. Guide the group to think about whether that seems surprising.

- **Question:** How does worship seem to connect to prayer?

  In your discussion, help the group pay attention to the ways the Campbells responded to what they felt was God's "calling forth" worship from their country.

- **Question:** Owen identifies a progression of changes in attitude among national believers in their attitude toward Muslim neighbours. What was that progression?

  Consider this: A segment of the national Christian population seemed to move from feeling like a persecuted underdog who don't care about their neighbours' spiritual well-being to being dedicated to reaching out to their neighbours.

- **Question:** What do the Campbells point out as an apostle's main two ministries?

  In your discussion, ask the group to consider the implications of Acts 6:4.

Make it personal

For the exercise to be beneficial to your group, you will need to see whether you can apply any of the fruitful practices to your own situation. Here are some questions to help your group make it personal.

- What do you find to be challenging in this narrative?
- Owen describes the period without fruit as a time of testing. Why do you think "the tap turned off"? Have you experienced similar periods? What has been the outcome?
- In what ways are you intentionally and strategically praying for Muslims?
- How could you network with others in this area?

Discussion: The Messiah Is Not a Liar

To prepare beforehand, the leader should follow the steps outlined on page 117.

Some fruitful practices you may note in this story

As a leader, be ready to highlight the following practices during the discussion. Research has shown these practices to be correlated with fruitfulness across a wide variety of ministry situations among Muslims.

- **Seekers 1**: Fruitful workers are bold in witness.
- **Seekers 3**: Fruitful workers pray for the needs of their friends in their presence.
- **Believers 4**: Fruitful workers help seekers and believers find appropriate ways to identify themselves to their community as followers of Jesus, without imposing their own preferences.
- **Believers 8**: Fruitful workers encourage believers to follow the Holy Spirit's leading in applying the Bible to their context.
- **Communication 7**: Fruitful workers share the gospel in ways that fit the learning preferences of their audience.

Observe and consider

- **Question**: What stood out most to you in this story? How did this story make you feel? What did it make you think about?

- **Question**: Why do you think Shaykh Musa kept telling people that Isa al Masih is not a liar?

  Possible answers include: What Isa al Masih prophesied came true.

- **Question**: What do you notice about how the believers are learning how to follow Jesus?

  In your discussion, help the group pay attention to the use of stories, the emphasis on obedience to God's Word, and the opportunity the believers gave God's Word to confront their cultural habits and beliefs.

- **Question**: How would you describe the way other villagers view the believers?

  Possible answers include: The other villagers seem to see the believers as people whose lives have changed, people who have access to spiritual power, people who view Abraham as the father of a faith that is fulfilled in Isa al Masih.

Make it personal

For the exercise to be beneficial to your group, you will need to see whether you can apply any of the fruitful practices to your own situation. Here are some questions to help your group make it personal.

- What do you find challenging in this story?
- How was the religious and societal situation in this story different from where you live? What difference does that make for your situation?

- What is the learning preference (oral or literate) of the people to whom you are giving witness? How should that affect your witness?
- What in this story sparked ideas for your ministry?
- Do you know anyone like Musa who could lead a group that gathers to pray and talk about the Bible and its effect in their lives?

Discussion: Stoking the Home Fire

To prepare beforehand, the leader should follow the steps outlined on page 117.

Some fruitful practices you may note in this story

As a leader, be ready to highlight the following practices during the discussion. Research has shown these practices to be correlated with fruitfulness across a wide variety of ministry situations among Muslims.

- **Society 5**: Fruitful workers pursue language proficiency.
- **Believers 1**: Fruitful workers are intentional in their discipling.
- **Believers 6**: Fruitful workers encourage believers to develop healthy relationships with other believers.
- **Believers 11**: Fruitful workers model service to others and teach believers to serve others as well.
- **Leaders 1**: Fruitful workers acknowledge emerging leaders early in the process of building a community of faith.
- **Leaders 2**: Fruitful workers mentor leaders who in turn mentor others.
- **Leaders 3**: Fruitful workers encourage leadership based on godly character.
- **Leaders 4**: Fruitful workers are intentional about leadership development.
- **Leaders 6**: Fruitful workers prefer to develop leaders locally.

- **Faith Communities 5**: Fruitful faith communities are committed to one another as extended family, practicing the biblical "one another" commands.

Observe and consider

- **Question**: What stood out most to you in this story? How did this story make you feel? What did it make you think about?

- **Question**: What was the crisis in this story and what led up to it?

    Possible answers include: The crisis came as the church dwindled to very low numbers. This crisis pushed Jack deeper in his intimacy with God, and it encouraged him to seek God for the answers he needed.

- **Question**: What did Jack do to develop local leadership among the followers of Jesus? What worked best and what did not?

    Possible answers include: He identified potential leaders quickly, mentored them intentionally, focused on character development, and trained them locally. He eventually learned that he also needed to model godly leadership.

- **Question**: How did Jack survive and adjust? What contributed to his family's resilience?

    Possible answers include: They learned the language. They connected closely with local people as friends. They submitted themselves to mentors to be held accountable.

- **Question**: Jack wanted to respect and honour the local culture, but this was not always straightforward. In what ways do you see him honouring the culture? In what ways did he challenge it? What were the ways that this was hard for Jack to discern?

    Possible answers include: Jack understood the role of hospitality, taking time to host people in his home and drink tea with them, giving the gift of time. He wanted the local culture to be reflected in the music of the church (and other expressions). He challenged the culture's norms of how to teach and how to resolve conflict. In the decision of whether or not to hold large public meetings, Jack had a more difficult time discerning what was appropriate.

- **Question**: What contributes to the health of this community?

    Possible answers include: Everyone who joins is expected to participate in a "Bible family," with committed relationships for prayer and accountability.

- **Question**: What was the most effective thing Jack did?

    Possible answers include: Learning the culture, living transparently, and teaching others to do the same, seeking God for an unusual answer and then following through on it, modelling servant leadership. Discuss why each person's answer means the most to him or her.

Make it personal

For the exercise to be beneficial to your group, you will need to see whether you can apply any of the fruitful practices to your own situation. Here are some questions to help your group make it personal.

- What did you find challenging?
- How was the religious and societal situation in this story different from where you live? What difference does that make for your situation?
- What in this story sparked ideas for your ministry?
- We all have blind spots, and it seems Jack's was not being able to hear the local leaders' arguments about large group meetings and his leadership. How do you discover and overcome your blind spots?

Discussion: Uncle, Is It True?

To prepare beforehand, the leader should follow the steps outlined on page 117.

Some fruitful practices you may note in this story

As a leader, be ready to highlight the following practices during the discussion. Research has shown these practices to be correlated with fruitfulness across a wide variety of ministry situations among Muslims.

- **Society 2:** Fruitful workers address tangible needs in their community as an expression of the gospel.

- **Society 7:** Fruitful workers build positive relationships with local leaders.

- **Seekers 2:** Fruitful workers pray for God's supernatural intervention as a sign that confirms the gospel.

- **Seekers 3:** Fruitful workers pray for the needs of their friends in their presence.

- **Seekers 4:** Fruitful workers share the gospel through existing social networks.

- **Believers 2:** Fruitful workers disciple in locally appropriate and reproducible ways.

- **Believers 9:** Fruitful workers encourage believers to share their faith.

- **Leaders 1:** Fruitful workers acknowledge emerging leaders early in the process of building a community of faith.

- **Leaders 4**: Fruitful workers are intentional about leadership development.
- **Communication 5**: Fruitful workers sow broadly.
- **Communication 7**: Fruitful workers share the gospel in ways that fit the learning preferences of their audience.
- **Faith Communities 4**: Fruitful faith communities value networking together.
- **Faith Communities 13**: Fruitful faith communities govern themselves.

Observe and consider

- **Question**: What stood out most to you in this story? How did this story make you feel? What did it make you think about?

- **Question**: In what ways did you see God intervening to confirm the truth of the gospel message?

    Possible answers include: God intervened miraculously in Hassan's healing, the conception of Ibrahim's child, and the destruction of the iron shirt. He also confirmed his truth through the lives of the foreigners who endured hardship and hostility in order to bring the gospel to the people. Yusuf's authentic life gained respect in his community, even among those who don't agree with him, which also served to confirm the gospel truth.

- **Question:** In what ways did you see the workers address tangible needs in the community as an expression of the gospel?

  Possible answers include: Foreigners started an NGO that gives relief to women and children. Yusuf started an affordable school that maintains high standards

- **Question:** What do you notice about how the believers make decisions and grow as disciples together?

  Possible answers include: They are learning to make decisions as a leadership group. The foreigners are gently pushing them in this direction, in anticipation of the day when they will have to leave. The believers are learning to encourage one another in faith.

- **Question:** What do you notice about how the believers share their faith?

  Possible answers include: They are bold in witness. They focus on family clans and relational networks. They use appropriate learning styles; for example, they tell stories since theirs is an oral culture.

Make it personal

For the exercise to be beneficial to your group, you will need to see whether you can apply any of the fruitful practices to your own situation. Here are some questions to help your group make it personal.

- What do you find challenging in this story?

- Which principles illustrated in this story might apply to your context?
- How could you tangibly address the needs of your community as an expression of the gospel?
- How are you helping local believers to make decisions and grow as disciples?

Fruitful Practices
A Descriptive List

by Fruitful Practice Research with John Becker, Eric Adams, and Laura Adams

Introduction

Have you ever faced a challenge and felt in your heart that "someone must have faced this before"? Did you end up solving your problem by yourself? In our common calling, we often discover that we have "reinvented the wheel" and repeated mistakes that others already have made – and learned from – before us. Why do we seem reluctant to learn from others and why don't our fellow workers share what they know?

We often speak of being good stewards of time, money, people and resources. Rarely, however, do we talk about being good stewards of our experience, especially the insight and knowledge we gain from watching the Father work in, through, and around us. Practicing good stewardship of knowledge would actually allow us to use our precious time,

---

Parts of this article have been previously published as Allen 2008, Woodberry 2008, 100-102, and Allen et al. 2009. This list has been jointly authored by members of Fruitful Practice Research. Eric Adams and Laura Adams have led that team during the research and development of the list of fruitful practices. John Becker, who shaped the introduction and has added reflective questions to this version, served in East Africa and England the past 15 years. He loves helping others fulfil their call to love Muslim people.

resources, and energy more effectively. We spend much of our time and resources re-learning key lessons that someone elsewhere has already learned.

More significantly, we can learn habits of equipping one another by sharing the best of our experience. Intentionally learning from and sharing from our experience increases fruitfulness across our common calling. It is our responsibility and privilege to be good stewards of the experience and knowledge that God has entrusted to us.

This list of 68 fruitful practices is the result of a multi-year, multi-agency study. In this context, "fruitful practices" refer to activities that promote the emergence, vitality, and multiplication of fellowships of Jesus's followers in a Muslim context. This document offers short descriptions of those practices that, through our study, have been correlated with "fruitful" efforts.

We call these practices "fruitful" rather than "best" or "good" because they bear life; they produce growth and reproduction. They have value beyond being worthy and commendable. We present this list as a starting point for the ongoing and important discussion of what indeed contributes to fruitfulness, based on the realities of experience and the foundation of scripture.

Read these practices carefully. Many of the principles listed here may be common sense, but they are not always common practice. Reflect on what is relevant in your context from this rich harvest of wisdom, then share what you've learned with someone else.

Research and Analysis. Rather than hypothesizing about which practices are most fruitful, the research team initially surveyed and interviewed effective teams from 13 organizations representing more than 5800 workers in the Muslim world. Then, in 2007, they recorded 100 interviews and collected notes from 25 discussion groups that met daily throughout a five-day consultation. Together, this produced more than 300 responses from individuals experienced in planting fellowships and representing over 30 organizations, two-thirds of which have witnessed the emergence of at least one Christ-centred community in the Muslim world.

Benchmarking. This approach seeks to develop a benchmark from inductive methods, discovering what God is currently using to grow his kingdom among Muslims in order to better partner with him in sowing and reaping. This approach differs significantly from a deductive method that follows the anecdotes and practices of a particular leader, seminary, or missiological theory. After research and analysis, a multi-agency team combed through results in order to clarify this list.

Cooperating with God. This process is our imperfect attempt to understand the mystery of ministry. All true ministries involve God's part and our part. We cannot change the heart of people. That is God's part. But we can share the gospel and demonstrate Christ's love. That is our part. (1 Corinthians 3:5-7 illustrates that dynamic: "What, after all, is Apollos? And what is Paul? Only servants, through whom you came to believe – as the Lord has assigned to each his task. I planted the seed, Apollos watered it, but God made it grow. So neither he who plants nor he who waters is anything, but only God, who makes things grow.")

Listening to what field workers are experiencing as fruitful practices can give us more clarity as we try to do our part to invite Muslims to follow Jesus. This list summarizes certain principles and practices multiple field workers have observed as being means that God is blessing and using to accomplish his purposes. It can point us in a direction that has great potential to bear fruit for his glory. When our faces are turned to the Father and his good work, the rest is up to him!

As you approach this list, please keep the following in mind:

- **Descriptive, not prescriptive.** This list is not a set of formulas to follow. Instead, we offer descriptions of the important features of the practice. You must always apply your own knowledge of local conditions as you prayerfully adapt these practices to work in your own context.

- **Evolving.** This list represents the "learning edge" for field workers – the facets of this work that seem to be most in need of focus at present. Staying attuned to what leads (and does not lead) to fruitfulness is a lifelong process of discovery. The list is by no means exhaustive. Certainly, there are gaps. Over time, as we tap into the insights of more field workers, representing the true range of nationalities and genders and field contexts, we will revise the current set. You play a crucial part in this process: Sharing practical knowledge is essential in our work. We hope this project will inspire field workers and agencies to adopt the habit of regularly taking time to review how God is working in and through them, and to share insights more intentionally within and among agencies.

- **Holistic.** These practices are mutually reinforcing. They contribute to fruitfulness as they remain in relationship with each other. This is especially true of practices within a particular category. The evidence from field data demonstrates that fruitfulness occurred with clusters of practices, not with any particular practice in isolation from the others.

- **The "God factor."** Think of this list as a summary of many ways we see God working through teams. These are practices that teams have found help them work with what God is doing.

Categorization

For ease of understanding, the practices are grouped into eight basic categories and each practice is labelled for ease of reference. Note that the order does not imply precedence or importance.

Category	Label
Relating to Society	Society
Relating to Believers	Believers
Relating to God	God
Fruitful Teams	Teams
Relating to Seekers	Seekers
Relating to Leaders	Leaders
Communication Methods	Communication
Characteristics of Fruitful Faith Communities	Faith Communities

Relating to Society

Without appropriate and ever-deepening relationships with Muslims in the context of their own community, how will a worker be a catalyst for the emergence of a faith community? The desire for this kind of open door into a Muslim society flows from the compelling love of Christ energizing the hearts of his workers. (See 2 Corinthian 5:14.)

This category of fruitful practices, "*Relating to Society,*" refers to the relationships that workers have with members of the society they encounter frequently or live within as they carry out their ministry. Oxford Dictionaries Online defines "society" as "the aggregate of people living together in a more or less ordered community" or "a particular community of people living in a country or region, and having shared customs, laws, and organizations." Although these fruitful practices relate to the specific Muslim community where a worker lives, they can also apply to the broader culture of a country or region.

The Bible uses the imagery of aliens or strangers when speaking of the position of believers in the world. (See Hebrews 11:13, 1 Peter 2:11.) The Apostle Paul adds a positive dimension to this position, calling those who are ministers of reconciliation "Christ's ambassadors" (2 Corinthians 5:19-20). These descriptions are especially apt when we speak of the cross-cultural worker. An ambassador is not only an alien but also a representative specifically chosen for a particular context. Guests who do not respect customs, laws, and traditions of their hosts are ungrateful and usually unwelcome guests.

Active appreciation for the local culture is at the heart of this group of practices. Workers will demonstrate this appreciation as they adopt an observant learning attitude and adapt their lifestyle appropriately. Pursuing proficiency in the host language(s) is a significant way workers demonstrate this appreciation. The fruitful worker is able to communicate effectively. The path to this fluency requires humility and perseverance.

Another way workers can express a learning attitude is to pursue partnership with the wider network of those seeking to bless the host people – through mobilizing prayer and learning from others who have researched or worked among the host people.

It is one thing to gain access to a society. It is much harder to maintain residency long enough to gain language fluency and build trusting relationships. The integrity of a worker's identity is crucial. Fruitfulness usually results from:

- Seeking to develop positive relationships with local leaders (for example, those who control who is "in" and who is "out")
- Having a valid reason for being present in the community
- Contributing to the society in relevant and tangible ways
- Making it clear that this contribution is an expression of the Gospel

Ask yourself about relating to society

- Which principles in God's Word can help shape my values and aspirations for how I relate to this society and its leadership?

- What would describe my relationship with the local society at present? (Or how do I hope my relationship with the local society will be described after I have lived there for a year?)
- How many of the values reflected in the statements below are evident in my attitudes and lifestyle?
- Which of my lifestyle choices might be hindering me from embracing these values?
- What resources are available that will give me the necessary insights into what this society values and how it operates?
- What are the specific actions I need to take to more fully live out these fruitful practices in relationship with this society?
- What are the specific actions I (and my co-workers) need to take to more fully live out these fruitful practices in relationship with this society?

Label	Practice and Description
Society 1	**Fruitful workers communicate respect by behaving in culturally appropriate ways.**
	A worker's attitude toward the host culture sends powerful messages. Fruitful workers behave in culturally appropriate ways in major cultural domains such as clothing and food, and especially in regards to hospitality. The key is sensitivity to the local setting, not necessarily whole-hearted adoption of local practice.

Label	Practice and Description
Society 2	**Fruitful workers address tangible needs in their community as an expression of the gospel.**
	Good deeds often help workers gain a good reputation in the host community. Fruitful workers make clear that their good deeds are an expression of the gospel; otherwise, local people may assume that the worker is simply a good person or is trying to earn religious merit.
Society 3	**Fruitful workers relate to people in ways that respect gender roles in the local culture.**
	Gender roles, and the taboos associated with them, are potent issues in the Muslim world. While maintaining a biblical perspective on these issues, fruitful workers strive to understand gender roles in their local context and demonstrate respect for these social norms.
Society 4	**Fruitful workers mobilize extensive, intentional, and focused prayer.**
	Fruitful workers invite others to join them through committed intercession for themselves and the people they are engaging. They recognize that this can be as important as inviting people to join the team that lives in the host culture.

Label	Practice and Description
Society 5	**Fruitful workers pursue language proficiency.**

Workers who are able to freely and clearly communicate in their host language(s) are much more likely to be fruitful. Fruitful workers carefully consider questions concerning language choice, such as whether to use heart or trade language, sacred or secular language. By learning language, they also gain a deeper understanding of culture, making language proficiency fruitful across a number of different dimensions.

Society 6	**Fruitful workers take advantage of pre-field and on-field research to shape their ministry.**

Fruitful ministry is shaped by many different streams of information, including ethnography, linguistics, and history. Workers who conduct research or actively reflect on the research of others are more fruitful than those who base their ministries on preconceived ideas or the patterns of ministry in their sending countries.

Label	Practice and Description
Society 7	**Fruitful workers build positive relationships with local leaders.** By sensitively and carefully relating to local authorities, including non-Christian religious figures, workers gain respect and good standing in their host community. Those who are intentional about choosing their relationships with local leaders are more likely to be fruitful.

Relating to Seekers

Scripture proclaims, "Anyone who trusts in him will never be put to shame." Scripture also promises, "Everyone who calls on the name of the Lord will be saved," but then asks, "How, then, can they call on the one they have not believed in? And how can they believe in the one of whom they have not heard? And how can they hear without someone preaching to them" (Romans 10:11-14)? This passage highlights the role of the worker as communicator of the gospel. The fruitful practices in this category have to do with the relationship between the workers and seekers as they intentionally communicate the gospel in word and deed.

We define a "seeker" as a Muslim who shows openness to the good news of Jesus. A seeker may be simply a person who hears or sees the gospel and sticks around to learn more or, at the other end of the spectrum, a person who has experienced Jesus or the gospel and is actively pursuing the truth.

Can seekers hear and see the gospel in your life and work? Boldness is fruitful, even though following Jesus and ministering in Muslim contexts is hemmed by challenges and restrictions. Fruitful workers live out their faith in tangible ways. They take the risk to boldly proclaim the power and work of Jesus.

"When a sown field is watered, the early stages of germination take place in the soil beneath the surface. This is also true of the process of emerging faith in the lives of our Muslim neighbours" (Woodberry 2008, 130). Recognizing this, the fruitful worker is intentional in his relationships and seeks to promote an environment in which faith can take root and grow. The fruitful worker, through personal example and word, teaches enquirers and seekers to obey the measure of God's truth they already understand.

Prayer is a key element in this category of practices. Prayer for members of the host people group, both in private and in public, is a practice of fruitful workers. What do they pray for? They pray for supernatural intervention in the lives of seekers. One fruitful worker shared, "We seek every opportunity we can to pray with people" (Woodberry 2008, 120). This might be prayer for healing, prayer for family members, prayer for a revelation of Christ, prayer for deliverance, or prayer for their business. Praying communicates faith in God's power, demonstrates that power for the seeker, and allows the seeker to experience the presence of God. In addition, the habit of prayer fosters our own humble reliance on the guidance and power of God as we carry out this calling.

Jesus told the man delivered from many demons to go home and tell his family how much the Lord had done for him

(Mark 5:19). In the same way, the fruitful worker encourages seekers to share every step in their journey of faith and the work of God in their life with family and friends. In situations where seekers do so, our research frequently shows that larger numbers of people come to faith. The fruitful worker seeks ways to multiply the spread of the gospel message among these pre-existing networks of trust.

Ask yourself about relating to seekers

- What does God's Word illustrate about how the Father reveals himself to people?

- What are my current approaches to living out my faith among Muslims?

- How many of the values represented in the statements below are evident in my attitudes and actions at present?

- Do I believe God will work supernaturally in the lives of my friends? In what ways can my actions show that I expect him to divinely work in the lives of my friends?

- What does God's Word say about the point at which he considers people his followers? Which aspects of discipleship (when and how it happens) do I need to rethink?

- What can I do to learn more about what my friends already understand about God, to discover ways God is already at work in their lives?

- After I share God's word with someone, does he or she share it with others? What can I do to nurture faith in my friends in a way that spreads to their family and existing networks of friends?

Label	Practice and Description
Seekers 1	**Fruitful workers are bold in witness.**

Boldness means different things in different situations. Some take great risk simply to live in dangerous environments. Others require courage to speak openly about Jesus in hostile settings. Fruitful workers do not recklessly endanger themselves or others in order to be bold, but they reflect the God-enabled power to point to Jesus Christ, in word and deed, even in the face of opposition.

Seekers 2 — **Fruitful workers pray for God's supernatural intervention as a sign that confirms the gospel.**

A demonstration of God's power has been a key factor for many Muslims who have come to faith in Jesus Christ. Aware of this, many fruitful workers pray specifically for God to intervene through dreams, healing, deliverance from evil spirits, and other clear signs to confirm the truth of the gospel.

Label	Practice and Description
Seekers 3	**Fruitful workers pray for the needs of their friends in their presence.**
	Fruitful workers display empathy for their friends by praying for them in their presence and not just in private. No matter how God answers, the worker who openly prays illustrates that God is concerned for daily needs and that he is the source of blessing and wholeness.
Seekers 4	**Fruitful workers share the gospel through existing social networks.**
	Group disapproval can be a significant barrier to any kind of social change. Group affirmation can be a significant catalyst that helps many people come to faith. In situations where many are coming to faith, often the impact and spread of the workers' initial witness has been multiplied as new believers share their faith with their family and community.

Label	Practice and Description
Seekers 5	**Fruitful workers begin discipling seekers as part of the process of coming to faith.**
	Fruitful workers recognize that not all seekers will become mature disciples of Jesus. Although there is wisdom in appropriate caution, they follow Jesus' example by helping those who express interest in him to hear and observe what it means to follow him.
Seekers 6	**Fruitful workers encourage seekers to share what God is doing in their lives.**
	The woman at the well of Sychar spontaneously told her fellow villagers about Jesus (John 4). Fruitful workers encourage seekers to find natural ways to talk with others about what God is doing for them and to invite them to "come and see the man ..."

Relating to Believers

This category includes the second greatest number of practices. It covers the where, when, how and with whom aspects of discipling believers. These practices are concerned with the relationship between the worker and the emerging followers of Jesus within the Muslim community. (See Romans 1:5.)

This category could be summarized by intentionality and sensitivity. Intentionality – because the fruitful worker is proactive about things such as encouraging believers to share their journey of faith with their family and network of relationships, and facilitating believers as they build relationships with one another, meeting up for teaching and encouragement. They also help believers consider their new identity in society. Sensitivity – because in all of this the fruitful worker takes into consideration the believer's culture, specific needs and potential for fruitfulness. Encouraging the believer towards obedience to the Holy Spirit and God's word, the fruitful worker is careful not to push his or her own biases.

While being intentional, the fruitful worker plans ahead and applies cultural knowledge to discipleship issues. The resources and methodology he or she uses are appropriate to the culture and are readily available for the believer to use with someone else. In learning how to do this, the fruitful worker is willing to try many approaches, and evaluate the outcomes. In planning where and how discipling will take place, decisions about such things as location and frequency are worked out together with the believer who ultimately has to live with the consequences (Woodberry 2008, 136).

The fruitful worker prepares believers to "give an answer" in order for them to explain their faith, develop their new identity as followers of Jesus and deal with persecution. (See 1 Peter 3:15.)

Life on life is another way to describe what leads to fruitfulness in discipling. The worker is vulnerable and intentionally lives out obedience to Christ, such as in serving others. This 'life on life' is a natural discipleship process which lends itself to modelling the lifestyle of a follower of Christ. How a disciple lives in the home, at work, at school, in business, in relating to the opposite sex, in dealing with authorities, etc. This approach to discipleship supports the idea that things such as values are better "caught than taught".

While learning cultural sensitivity, it is reproduction (or fruitfulness) in the believer's life that is of chief concern. Therefore, the fruitful worker nurtures such things as:

- dependence on the Holy Spirit
- the application of the Word of God
- continuance with their family and social networks
- connectivity with other believers

One example of this is in relation to baptism where fruitfulness is found when baptism is administered by others with a Muslim background.

Accountability is a critical dimension in encouraging obedience and correcting waywardness. Fruitfulness is seen when exhortation is both biblical and contextual.

Essential in all of these practices relating to believers is a love for the individual–while recognizing that every individual is vitally connected with family and other trust networks. Why such care in discipling, protecting, encouraging, living alongside? It is because "Jesus Christ laid down his life for us. And we ought to lay down our lives for our brothers" (1 John 3:16).

Ask yourself about relating to believers

- What does God's Word teach about his goals for discipleship relationships?

- What best describes my discipleship efforts? Are they proactive or reactive?

- What factors or information have shaped the approaches I am currently using? (Ministry in other contexts? Insights from other workers? Observations in the current context?) When I consider discipleship principles, what cultural biases might be influencing my opinions?

- How many of the values represented in the statements are evident in my current approaches?

- In which areas do I need to develop more intentionality?

- In which areas do I need to develop greater sensitivity?

- Are those whom I disciple teaching others? What aspects of my discipleship approaches can believers do without my help or resources? What can they not do without my help or resources?

Label	Practice and Description
Believers 1	**Fruitful workers are intentional in their discipling.**

Jesus calls his followers to train disciples to obey all that he commanded. Disciples are made, not born. Disciple-making does not occur by accident. Fruitful workers provide intentional guidance, encouragement, and exhortation so that disciples will grow in maturity and obedience.

Believers 2	**Fruitful workers disciple in locally appropriate and reproducible ways.**

Disciples are more likely to share their faith and make new disciples when all needed books, tools, and resources are locally available. Fruitful workers avoid relying on discipleship manuals that must be ordered from abroad, electronic equipment that is unaffordable for disciples, or training that is only offered elsewhere.

Label	Practice and Description
Believers 3	**Fruitful workers disciple others in settings that fit the situation.**
	When meeting with disciples, fruitful workers are deliberate about the location, time, and circumstance. They know that these factors have an effect on the disciple's availability and readiness for reflection. For example, it is likely to be more appropriate for women to disciple women in homes during the day. Workers take advantage of every opportunity, both unplanned as well as planned (shopping at the bazaar, or meeting for Bible study). Finally, they look for ways to engage with more than one disciple at the same time.
Believers 4	**Fruitful workers help seekers and believers find appropriate ways to identify themselves to their community as followers of Jesus, without imposing their own preferences.**
	Fruitful workers actively help seekers and believers to consider ways to establish their identity in their community by asking them questions that help them consider their alternatives. They avoid presuming or predetermining this identity for followers of Jesus.

Label	Practice and Description
Believers 5	**Fruitful workers help believers find ways to remain within their social network.**

Most seekers and believers live in strong webs of existing family, social and religious relationships. The gospel is more likely to spread quickly when faith travels through these existing webs. Fruitful workers encourage seekers and believers to maintain these relationships, to share their faith journey with family and friends and to incorporate new seekers and believers into fellowships within those networks.

Believers 6	**Fruitful workers encourage believers to develop healthy relationships with other believers.**

Seekers and believers need to know that they are not the only ones in their society or family who follow Jesus. Fruitful workers help seekers and believers live in unity by obeying the New Testament commands such as "love one another," "serve one another," "honour one another," and "stop passing judgment on one another" (Romans 12:10, 16; 13:8; 14:13; Galatians 5:13; Ephesians 4:32 and others). Fruitful workers help believers to overcome divisive practices and attitudes such as revenge, jealousy, and gossip.

Label	Practice and Description
Believers 7	**Fruitful workers model following Jesus in intentional relationships with believers.**
	Fruitful workers recognize that discipleship is a relational process. While spending many hours with seekers and believers, they reveal their own faith journey. Whether they are drinking tea at a café or praying for the sick, fruitful workers find ways to share relevant biblical stories or teachings from the life of Jesus. Their goal is to demonstrate vibrant faith as a constant follower of Jesus and to coach the seeker and believer to do the same.
Believers 8	**Fruitful workers encourage believers to follow the Holy Spirit's leading in applying the Bible to their context.**
	Rather than imposing their own application and interpretation on biblical passages, fruitful workers help seekers and believers to ask for God's help as they reflect on biblical truth and apply it to their situation. They encourage seekers and believers to trust that God will answer them when they ask for his for help.

Label	Practice and Description
Believers 9	**Fruitful workers encourage believers to share their faith.**

Understanding that discipleship involves witness, fruitful workers motivate seekers and believers to tell others what God is doing in their lives. Believers are more likely to make new disciples when they begin, early in their faith journey, to share what they are learning from the Bible, how God answered their prayers, and what they are learning about Jesus.

Believers 10	**Fruitful workers prepare believers to explain why they believe.**

While sharing their faith with others in their social webs, seekers and believers often hear scepticism or arguments that raise doubt in their hearts. Fruitful workers strengthen their growing faith by helping them to explain their reasons for believing in Jesus. By anticipating these objections, the worker can share responses with the disciple using the Bible, scientific evidence, or the Quran. The worker's goal is the disciple's personal ownership of his or her faith.

Label	Practice and Description
Believers 11	**Fruitful workers model service to others and teach believers to serve others as well.**

In the everyday activities of life, fruitful workers intentionally serve others in every circumstance, explaining that this is how to live as a disciple of Jesus. They encourage seekers and believers to do the same, explaining that faith and good deeds go together. By integrating teaching and practice, they help the disciple to live authentically before a watching community so that the community experiences the goodness of Jesus.

Believers 12	**Fruitful workers use various approaches in discipling.**

Fruitful workers employ a variety of means while making disciples. For example, a group of disciples may see the Jesus film, experience prayer for healing, and participate in Bible study—all at the same time. Fruitful workers develop a toolbox of approaches and resources to use.

Label	Practice and Description
Believers 13	**Fruitful workers encourage baptism by other believers with a Muslim background.**

The most common method of baptism is an arranged event witnessed by Muslim background believers and sometimes seekers. Cross-cultural workers do not usually conduct the baptism but may be present. Fruitful workers recognise that baptism strengthens the sense of community among believers. Among emerging fellowships, the most common practice is believer's baptism by immersion.

Believers 14	**Fruitful workers deal with sin in biblical ways that are culturally appropriate.**

Fruitful workers understand that the biblical principles of correction of sin and restoration, as described in Matthew 18 and Galatians 6:1-2, must be applied within the local cultural context and world view. In the process of applying biblical teaching, fruitful workers consider local cultural dynamics such as honour and shame, gender roles, community standards, family and clan status, and social standing.

Relating to Leaders

Who chooses leaders? How do they select the leaders? What are the best leadership development tools? What contexts are best for leadership development?

The practices in this category address these questions and apply to choosing, appointing, preparing and reproducing leaders in the emerging faith community. Fruitful workers use the word of God as their central leadership development tool. They major on the Biblical text to identify and train leaders. The Bible clearly outlines leaders' qualities and godly character traits.

"A leader who has [negative] character issues will reproduce that in followers. Our character is the number one thing." This is how one group of workers expressed the importance of godly character in leaders. One of seven key characteristics of growing movements of communities of Muslim background believers is that leaders meet the 1 Timothy 3 and Titus 1 leadership criteria (Woodberry 2008, 161-162).

With a biblical view of leadership for the faith community, fruitful workers have their eyes and hearts tuned toward encouraging leaders to rise up from among the believers early on. They have a plan to empower recognized leaders and take care not to appoint people based on their own cultural biases. The fruitful worker asks, "What do godly leadership qualities look like in this culture?"

Whether it is in the way they use the Bible or the settings in which they carry out leadership development, fruitful workers make decisions with an understanding and appreciation of the local culture. They prepare leaders with the local context in mind and avoid sending them away to foreign training programs. Fruitful workers model leadership naturally through relationships and do not rely solely on formal or institutional programs. Occasionally, when the local context limits their development, the worker may send away for training certain leaders who have proven themselves locally first.

Following the biblical model of Paul and his training of Timothy (2 Timothy 2:2), fruitful workers expect the leaders they train to invest in others, and so on – creating an environment that empowers the ones God has gifted to impart these gifts to others.

Ask yourself about relating to leaders

- Which scriptures teach about leadership within the faith community? Which character traits and qualities are to be found in leaders? (1 and 2 Kings, 1 and 2 Timothy, and Titus are good places to start.)
- What are the differences in the ways that leadership is perceived and expressed in my home culture and this host culture? In what ways do I need to rethink leadership in light of these differences?
- How many of the values represented in the statements below are evident in my current approaches?
- Which leaders that I have been working with are also training others to lead?
- Which approaches that I am currently using are proving to be effective and reproducible? Which can be adapted? Which need to be discarded? How can I foster resources that emerge out of the local context?

In light of these discoveries, which leaders does God want me to invest in? What steps will I take to do this?

Label	Practice and Description
Leaders 1	**Fruitful workers acknowledge emerging leaders early in the process of building a community of faith.** Fruitful workers acknowledge the leaders who emerge naturally during the formation of a faith community. They support those who are recognized by the community rather than choosing leaders based on their own culturally developed understanding of leadership.
Leaders 2	**Fruitful workers mentor leaders who in turn mentor others.** A mentor passes on skills, character, and wisdom to a developing leader. Fruitful workers also guide the mentored leader to mentor others in the same way, as described in 2 Timothy 2:2.

Label	Practice and Description
Leaders 3	**Fruitful workers encourage leadership based on godly character.**

Leaders in fruitful, expanding communities meet the criteria that focus on godly character described in 1 Timothy 3 and Titus 1. While such communities select their own leaders, fruitful workers support and encourage the community by looking for emerging leaders with godly character.

Leaders 4	**Fruitful workers are intentional about leadership development.**

Leadership development should be intentional, but its format is often non-formal. Fruitful workers provide personalized leadership development in one-on-one, natural settings, rather than in classrooms.

Leaders 5	**Fruitful workers use the Bible as the primary source for leadership development.**

Fruitful workers do not depend on outside resources to develop leaders, as these rarely apply to the local context, they are not easily transferable, and they lack the authority of scripture. Instead, fruitful workers use scripture as the primary source for leadership development. To do so requires a thorough understanding of the local culture.

Label	Practice and Description
Leaders 6	**Fruitful workers prefer to develop leaders locally.**
	Fruitful workers prefer to develop leaders as locally as possible. If it is not possible to train leaders geographically locally, then it is more fruitful to train leaders within local culture and local social norms. When leaders are trained outside of the local setting, they can find it difficult to return. The further their training is from local life, the less likely it is that they will return and readjust well.

Relating to God

The foundation for fruitfulness for workers is their own personal relationship with God. From this flows everything else. Jesus says this relationship can only exist if we abide in (remain vitally connected to) him. He makes a wonderful promise to us – as we persist in abiding in him, we will bear much fruit, and this fruit will last. In Jesus's discourse to his disciples in John 15:1-5, there is a progression from "fruit" to "more fruit" to "much fruit." The intent is that we have been chosen to bear much lasting fruit that has lasting value. This particular fruit relates both to enduring character transformation in us and also to the impact of our lives on others.

What does it look like to "abide" (or "remain connected to God")? This section has to do with the workers' walk with God. Fruitful workers are determined to stay connected to their life source. It is an active priority. Alone, they will neither last nor bear meaningful fruit. But they will keep in community with Christ as they discipline themselves and walk in the same manner as him. Paul writes that the works of a true apostle are done with perseverance (2 Corinthians 12:12). James reminds us that the finished work of perseverance in us brings maturity and completion (James 1:4).

Perseverance is grounded in an experience of God's grace. Fruitful workers have counted the cost and persevere through trials without retreating to safer environments. They tap into the grace of God to supply all they need. They echo Paul's words to the Colossians, "I rejoice in what was suffered for you, and I fill up in my flesh what is still lacking in regard to Christ's afflictions, for the sake of his body, which is the church" (Colossians 1:24).

Ask yourself about relating to God

- What does God in his Word say about the relationship he desires with me?
- What characterizes the way I relate with God at present?
- Which values in the Word and in the statements below are evident in my current way of relating with God?
- Which areas do I neglect in my relationship with God? What factors contribute to this? (Which excuses do I find myself using?)
- Which aspects of my prayer life need growth? What might help me grow in this?

- What impact might changes in my spiritual walk have on my ministry?
- How have I been demonstrating perseverance? What will help me to persevere in my ministry?
- What might my willingness to persevere communicate to those to whom I am ministering?

Label	Practice and Description
God 1	**Fruitful workers practice an intimate walk with God.** Fruitful workers value and cultivate their responsiveness to God. Intimacy implies heart level, two-way communication in the midst of busyness and stress. Their relationship with God is based not on religious behaviour, but on daily honest interaction with him.
God 2	**Fruitful workers engage in regular, frequent prayer.** Fruitful workers say that prayer, whether corporate or individual, has been of high value to them. They dedicate time and attention to prayer.
God 3	**Fruitful workers persevere through difficulty and suffering.** Fruitful workers remain with their host people, enduring through suffering and difficulties.

Communication Methods

Our desire as workers is not only that the gospel should reach the ears and eyes of Muslims, but also that it should penetrate their hearts. This category's focus is the effective communication of the gospel.

Effective communication is a two-way process: when all goes well, one side sends a message, and the other side receives and understands the message as it was intended. Recognizing that people communicate in a variety of ways, fruitful workers use various approaches in order to communicate life giving truth successfully to Muslims. Variety is evident in the range of methods fruitful workers use, including:

- doing investigative Bible studies
- relating the truth via proverbs and stories
- distributing literature
- using life and community events as opportunities for gospel messages
- broadcasting via radio, television and film
- doing acts of mercy and kindness
- demonstrating God's power to heal and set people free

The scope of ministry efforts also demonstrates this variety – from wide-reaching activities that allow the gospel to be heard by as many ears as possible to one-on-one personal sharing in a way that affects family and social networks.

Fruitful workers use methods, activities, and evangelistic tools that are reproducible locally so that the believers and the growing faith community can use them in their own outreach efforts. This is reminiscent of what Paul testified to when writing to the church in Thessalonica. He reminded the believers that the gospel did come to them "in word only, but also with power, with the Holy Spirit and with deep conviction." The impact was that they became imitators of their messengers and of the Lord and were an example to other believers, which spread the gospel even further. (See 1 Thessalonians 1:5-8.)

Whatever the method, the fruitful worker ensures that the gospel is being communicated effectively. In most situations, workers are fruitful when they use the heart language of the people. Determining which language is most appropriate for communicating the good news requires wisdom. But there are more issues to consider as well. Communicating effectively also requires understanding and using the learning preferences of the host culture as well, especially in oral societies. For example, many fruitful workers reported that oral storytelling approaches had proven to be very effective. For example, they often used thematic stories that responded to felt needs as they arose. "The Lord would bring up felt needs, then there would be a story from scripture, ... [about] who is Jesus and who is God, what is His character, what is His nature..." They found that using stories was "a real freeing approach" with people who would never have accepted a printed copy of the Bible, but who enjoyed the stories (Burke 2008, 51).

What kind of people do we serve? What are their concerns? What are the significant symbols and values of their culture? Do we know their "story" – how they experience life? Fruitful workers address questions like these as they explore the most effective ways to communicate the gospel (Woodberry 2008, 113). They trust and use the word of God, emphasizing relevant scripture to allow Muslims to experience the heart of God. This might extend even to the presentation of the scriptures in styles and formats that appeal to and are acceptable to the Muslim audience. In doing so, they exhibit both a command of the Bible and insight into the local culture.

In Acts 17:22-34, Paul effectively used the writings of Greek philosophers Epimenides and Aratus to bridge to truth about God to the Epicurean and Stoic philosophers in Athens. Similarly, fruitful workers use portions of the Quran as a bridge to enable Muslims to discover the truth about God and salvation.

Ask yourself about communication methods

- In God's Word, what range of ways does God use to communicate truth to people? Compare this with some of the values reflected in the statements below.
- What have been the primary methods of communication God has used to penetrate my heart?
- What is the preferred means of communicating spiritual truths in my host culture? How does this differ from the preferred means of communicating in my own culture?
- How might I redeem local communication practices for gospel witness?
- What are ways that I can listen more deeply to the lives of my friends, to understand the content of and ways they relate their "stories"?

- Story telling is an effective means of communication. What stories, including the one that describes my own journey of faith, might God want me to master in the language of the Muslims with whom I am sharing?
- Considering the various approaches I use to share the gospel, what characterizes the approaches I have chosen so far?
- How widely am I sharing? Do I communicate only one-on-one or also to broader groups?

Label	Practice and Description
Communication 1	**Fruitful workers use culturally appropriate Bible passages to communicate God's message.**
	The Bible is central in the communication of God's message, but using it effectively requires cultural insight. Fruitful workers help seekers find the passages that address the issues most relevant to them. The ability to effectively apply biblical truth to the issues of life requires a thorough knowledge of God's word and an ongoing dependence on wisdom from God.

Label	Practice and Description
Communication 2	**Fruitful workers communicate the gospel using the heart language, except in situations where it is not appropriate.**
	In most situations, the heart language is undoubtedly the best way to meaningfully communicate the gospel. However, in areas where more than one language is in common use, established patterns often dictate when one language should be used as opposed to another. Fruitful workers seek to understand local patterns of language use and plan their communication strategies accordingly.
Communication 3	**Fruitful workers use a variety of approaches in sharing the gospel.**
	No one method of gospel communication covers every need and will always be the most effective. Often the best approach to sharing the gospel depends on the audience and the situation in question. Fruitful workers learn to use a variety of different approaches and apply them as appropriate to the setting.

Label	Practice and Description
Communication 4	**Fruitful workers share the gospel using tools or methods that can be locally reproduced.**
	In order for faith communities to grow without hindrance, the members of the communities must have access to all the tools they need in their local context. For this reason, fruitful workers focus on methods for sharing the gospel that require only tools and resources that are readily available in the local community.
Communication 5	**Fruitful workers sow broadly.**
	It is not possible to know in advance which ground will bear the most fruit. Fruitful workers sow broadly and pray for wisdom to know where to invest time in personal relationships. They maintain an ongoing balance between the broad sowing of God's word and the time spent developing individual relationships.

Label	Practice and Description
Communication 6	**Fruitful workers use Bible study as a means of sharing the gospel.**

Spending time in the study of God's word allows seekers to discover God's truths for themselves. In some instances, fruitful workers may simply read the Bible with a seeker, responding to questions relating to the text as they arise. In other instances, they may tell Bible stories and ask questions to help seekers discover how to apply the stories to their lives.

Communication 7	**Fruitful workers share the gospel in ways that fit the learning preferences of their audience.**

Although people from western countries rely heavily on written media, people in many other parts of the world are accustomed to oral forms of communication. Good communicators understand the learning preferences of their audience and plan their communication strategies accordingly.

Label	Practice and Description
Communication 8	**Fruitful workers use the Quran as a bridge to sharing the biblical gospel.**
	Certain passages from the Quran can be used effectively in sharing the gospel. Discretion is needed, as inappropriate references to the Quran may validate a seeker's belief in the divine origin of the book. In general, the use of the Quran as a bridge is most advisable when relating to seekers who already know the Quran well. Fruitful workers do not dwell unnecessarily on the Quran, but use various passages as a bridge in order to share the biblical gospel.

Fruitful Teams

There are many ways to define "team." One helpful definition is: a small group of people committed to a common purpose, goals, and approach for which they hold themselves accountable (Becker 2008). The following category expands this definition through nine practices that describe fruitful teams of labourers ministering among Muslims.

Operating as a team, rather than on one's own, can itself be seen as a fruitful practice as it is certainly a biblical one. Teams model the body of Christ. But what has proven to be fruit-bearing within teams? The above definition highlights a key component of fruitful teams – common purpose, goal and approach. This shared "vision" is the fundamental reason for the team's existence. Clarity about this vision allows a team to move forward, focus on essentials, strengthen one another through interdependence, and by God's grace accomplish their goals. As they move forward, fruitful teams take time to evaluate and reassess and adapt their strategy appropriately. One practical tool some teams use is After Action Review.

Beyond sharing their vision, fruitful teams also lovingly affirm one another. Doing so strengthens each member, which increases the overall strength and effectiveness of the team. For example, members of a fruitful team may gently ask one another a question like, "Are you thriving or surviving?" This kind of accountability between team members enables concern and positive peer pressure to pull members out of rough patches.

Fruitful teams know and respect one another's gifts and abilities. This translates into interdependence. On fruitful teams, each member provides a unique contribution. There are no bystanders on fruitful teams. Each member not only has something to offer, but also is expected to participate, especially in sharing the gospel. Believers receive spiritual gifts and are expected to use them in the context of the body. Paul's teams were successful because Paul deployed them so as to be complementary in gifts and ministry. Paul never chose to work alone. He was always surrounded by co-workers, and he used them wisely (Dale 2008).

A recurring theme throughout the categories of fruitful practices is the importance of using the heart language of the host culture. One of the most consistent and significant practices of fruitful teams is that at least one member has a high proficiency in the heart language of the host people. Fruitful teams invest in learning and using the appropriate languages of the Muslim community they serve.

> *Two of the strongest associations with fruitfulness are that the workers are ministering in the local or "heart language" of the people to whom they were called, and that teams include at least one person who is highly fluent in the ministry language. While some participants noted that some workers seem to communicate effectively while speaking in a trade or regional language, the qualitative analysis indicates there was a far more likely chance of seeing mature fruit and/or multiplication of communities of faith when the gospel is proclaimed in the medium of the "heart language" (Adams, Allen and Fish 2009, 75-81).*

Central to teams' effectiveness is that they have clearly identified and gifted leadership. Fruitful teams have a leadership dynamic – one that develops and employs each member's strengths and abilities, nurtures the team as a body, and keeps it focused.

A "spiritual discipline" is the intentional turning of a specific part of one's way of life toward God. A spiritual discipline, when practiced faithfully and regularly, becomes a habit or regular pattern in one's life that repeatedly brings awareness back to God and enables one to listen to what God is saying. All believing communities should practice spiritual disciplines, but they are especially important for teams of God's ambassadors to Muslims (Dale 2008).

Fruitful teams practice spiritual disciplines to nurture their individual relationships with God. They also engage in corporate prayer and fasting. They love the communities they are serving, and they believe that God responds to prayer and sees the broken hearts of his people as they sacrifice for those he has called them to serve. They bow before God in order to hear his voice and discern his leading so they can follow to bear the fruit he has promised to them.

Ask yourself about your team

- What does God say in his Word about how he has designed members of Christ's body to operate well as a team? There are a number of task-oriented teams in the Bible (for example, the spies in Exodus, Jonathan and his armour bearer in 1 Samuel, Paul and Barnabas and various teams in Acts). Which of their qualities and characteristics are worth emulating in my team?

- What values in the principles listed below are evident in my team? Which areas need growth?

- What vision has God given me and my co-workers? How much do we all agree and "own" this vision?

- In what ways are we using our various gifts and abilities? What could enhance our ability to encourage and strengthen one another in order to become more effective in ministry?

- What hinders us most from growing in mutual respect and effective ministry? What are key ways that the enemy undermines our unity in Christ and our love for one another?

- Leaders: How might I better affirm and empower the members of my team towards greater effectiveness?
- How do we practice prayer and fasting as a team? How might we develop these vital corporate spiritual disciplines?

Label	Practice and Description
Teams 1	**Fruitful teams are united by a common vision.** Fruitful teams are comprised of members who share a common goal and strategy. This contrasts with teams on which many members are pursuing different goals – focusing on different people groups or different outcomes.
Teams 2	**Fruitful teams build one another up in love.** The members of fruitful teams develop life-giving relationships with one another. Such teams learn to affirm and respect one another's gifts and efforts, resolve conflicts honestly, and bear one another's burdens.
Teams 3	**Fruitful teams have effective leadership.** Teams with healthy leadership dynamics are teams on which the leaders catalyse the varied gifts of the members so that they are able to work together toward the team's goals.

Label	Practice and Description

Teams 4 **Fruitful teams employ the various gifts of their members to serve the task.**

Fruitful teams affirm the varied gifts of the members and encourage them to blossom. Team members are more fruitful when their gifts are deployed in roles and functions that best serve their vision for mission rather than on other projects.

Teams 5 **Fruitful teams adapt their methods based on reflective evaluation and new information.**

Teams bear fruit when they intentionally evaluate their progress. They change their methods and strategies when necessary. They adapt their methods based on the experience of informed local experts and other efforts to build God's kingdom.

Teams 6 **Fruitful teams have at least one person with high language proficiency in the heart language.**

Fruitful teams prioritize learning the heart language of their host people. They make sure all members are on the path toward greater involvement in the language community and value the members who attain high fluency in language and culture.

Label	Practice and Description
Teams 7	**Fruitful teams engage in corporate prayer and fasting.**
	Fruitful teams value and prioritize seeking God's ways through prayer and fasting together.
Teams 8	**Fruitful teams expect every team member to be involved in sharing the gospel.**
	Within fruitful teams, all team members view themselves as a means for God to communicate his truth and love to the host people. The members will have different personalities, gifting and daily job descriptions – from the mother of young children to the businessperson. But their interactions with host people are characterized by their availability to respond to God and reveal Jesus Christ through their character and witness. This contrasts with teams that expect only a few members to carry out the task of evangelism.
Teams 9	**Fruitful teams value their female members as essential partners in ministry, facilitating their active involvement.**
	Fruitful teams recognize the necessity for women to reach women with the gospel message. They help the women on the team to give energy and time to developing relationships and contributing their gifts. This contrasts with teams that regard their male team members as the primary workers.

Characteristics of Fruitful Faith Communities

Peter says,

> *But you are a chosen people, a royal priesthood, a holy nation, a people belonging to God, that you may declare the praises of him who called you out of darkness into his wonderful light. Once you were not a people, but now you are the people of God; once you had not received mercy, but now you have received mercy (1 Peter 2:9-10).*

Our goal is not just to proclaim the gospel or to see a few individuals enter the kingdom of God. Our purpose is nothing short of establishing naturally multiplying communities of believers who follow Jesus. These faith communities will eventually transform their own society and send out messengers to other nations.

The local church is the expression of God's transforming truth, power, character, and purposes. The most fruitful church plants have an identity firmly rooted in their own culture. These church plants are viable, attractive witnesses to the wider Muslim society. This might seem like common sense, but it is not always intuitive or common practice. Cross-cultural workers often do not realize the subtle ways they can influence the emerging community to develop in foreign and non-reproducible ways.

The church, grounded in its allegiance to God as king, provides a dramatic witness as God transforms a community of ordinary people. This community of faith is living proof to the surrounding Muslim society that the kingdom of God has come, breaking into their culture – in an incarnational, counter-cultural, yet distinctly "one of us" manner – to powerfully transform individuals and society. The members of fruitful faith communities are equipped to actively share their faith with others. This is electrifyingly good news to Muslims who spend their lives longing to please God, but often feeling that they fall short of what he wants of them.

This community of faith is the longed-for fruit of our ministry efforts. If established well, this community will remain long after cross-cultural workers have left. It will continue to multiply spontaneously, leavening the society with the blessings promised to Abraham, affecting other cultures as God calls out apostles and church planters to go from its midst to those yet unreached.

The church of Acts is not an oddity that merely existed for a brief while after Jesus's death. It is living and growing across the Muslim world today! The Word-become-flesh is bringing hearts to life and transforming lives. Divine power is breaking in to heal, satisfy needs, and restore relationships. Believers are taking courageous stands in hostile communities and winning the hearts of their neighbours by their acts of faith!

They are even taking this great story to neighbouring peoples. Muslims see God walking with friends and neighbours, people they know intimately. Their hearts are kindled with hope that he can walk alongside them, too.

Ask yourself about faith communities

- What examples do I see in God's Word about the relationship between faith communities and their surrounding society? What is God's intention for the impact or influence they can have?

- What values are evident in the list of practices below?
- What would characterize the faith communities in the host culture? (If none exist yet, what do I picture them as being like?)
- What are we doing that might be leading to the growth of these qualities in the faith community?
- What are we doing that might be stifle or inhibit the faith community from having these qualities?

Label	Practice and Description
Faith Communities 1	**Fruitful faith communities use the Bible as the central source for life, growth and mission.** In a culture where many books are viewed as holy, a fruitful faith community views and uses the Bible as the central source for their understanding of God and how to live their life as followers of Jesus.
Faith Communities 2	**Fruitful faith communities worship using indigenous forms of expression.** Fruitful faith communities design their worship using indigenous music and other forms of expression that reflect their cultural heritage, including prayer posture, seating arrangements, or the kinds of food used when sharing the Lord's Supper.

Label	Practice and Description
Faith Communities 3	**Fruitful faith communities practice baptism.**
	Baptism is practiced and understood in a variety of ways by the worldwide body of Christ. Whether it is full immersion or a sprinkling of water, at the beginning of a faith journey or as a milestone in an ongoing journey, baptism is a common practice in a fruitful faith community.
Faith Communities 4	**Fruitful faith communities value networking together.**
	Understanding that their community is part of the larger body of Christ, fruitful communities place a value on building trust and support with other faith communities. The circumstances of each community vary, but fruitful communities find ways to do things like fellowship together, train leaders together, or pray for one another.

Label	Practice and Description
Faith Communities 5	**Fruitful faith communities are committed to one another as extended family, practicing the biblical "one another" commands.**
	Jesus commandment to "love one another as I have loved you" challenges faith communities to reach beyond their families and come to understand other followers of Jesus as brothers and sisters in Christ. Fruitful faith communities embrace this command and put it into practice as they build relationships within their community.
Faith Communities 6	**Fruitful faith communities redeem traditional festivals and ceremonies.**
	Life cycle ceremonies (such as weddings and funerals, traditions surrounding birth and death, and festivals that mark various events in a culture's historical identity) are important to the fabric of any society. Rather than abandon all tradition or remove themselves from all association with traditional festivals, fruitful faith communities seek ways to redeem them as an expression of their faith in Jesus.

Label	Practice and Description
Faith Communities 7	**Fruitful faith communities share meals and practice hospitality.**
	Sharing meals and practicing hospitality are honourable traits in any culture. Jesus demonstrates that these are not only ways to gain honour but are also ways to love one another and to love neighbours. Fruitful faith communities seek to bless others and provide a witness to Jesus' love through their fellowship and generous hospitality.
Faith Communities 8	**Fruitful faith communities share the Lord's Supper in culturally appropriate ways.**
	Fruitful faith communities use elements and adopt a method of sharing the Lord's Supper that makes the most sense in their cultural context. In the West, the elements of bread and wine are commonly used. But in many cultures, bread is not available and wine is forbidden. Likewise, there are many ways to distribute the elements, either during a meal or as a separate service.

Label	Practice and Description
Faith Communities 9	**Fruitful faith communities seek to bless their wider community.** |//

Faith Communities 9 — **Fruitful faith communities seek to bless their wider community.**

One way to provide a witness to the truth of the gospel and build trust is to find ways to bless a community. Fruitful faith communities consider the needs in the community and seek to bless those who are outside their own faith community, whether through building a well, providing child care, conducting a medical clinic, or some other means.

Faith Communities 10 — **Fruitful faith communities involve women in culturally appropriate forms of ministry.**

Understanding that the Lord calls both men and women to participate in ministry, fruitful faith communities seek to involve women in ways that are appropriate for the cultural context. In some areas, this may be limited to hospitality. In others, it may be appropriate for a woman to serve the Lord's Supper or to lead other women in studying the Bible.

Label	Practice and Description
Faith Communities 11	**Fruitful faith communities involve their children in worship and ministry.**
	Children are not only the future of a faith community; they are its present as well. Fruitful faith communities actively involve their children, teaching them by example and giving them opportunities to grow in discipleship through worship and ministry.
Faith Communities 12	**Fruitful faith communities equip their members to share their faith in effective and culturally appropriate ways.**
	Believers share their faith in many ways. What is effective in some cultural settings may be counterproductive in others. Fruitful faith communities encourage their members to share their faith and equip them to do so in ways that are appropriate for the situation.

Label	Practice and Description
Faith Communities 13	**Fruitful faith communities govern themselves.**

Fruitful faith communities make their own decisions about direction, leadership, priorities, and practices. They take responsibility to build and rule their community of faith. Although they may provide coaching or counsel, fruitful workers step out of direct leadership as soon as multiple local leaders are prepared to take the lead.

Faith Communities 14	**Fruitful faith communities have local accountability structures for the use of funds.**

Whether the funds come from foreign or national sources, fruitful faith communities demonstrate direct responsibility and accountability for the use of funds.

Label	Practice and Description
Faith Communities 15	**Fruitful faith communities generally meet in homes or other informal settings.**
	One of the primary marks of a fruitful faith community is its ability to reproduce. As its community is defined, the emphasis is on the presence of believers and not the place where the believers meet. Rather than requiring worship or study to take place in a specific building, fruitful communities commonly encourage meetings in informal settings.

Works Cited

Adams, Eric, Don Allen, and Bob Fish. "Seven Themes of Fruitfulness." *International Journal of Frontier Missiology* 26, no. 2 (2009): 75-81.

Allen, Don. "Fruitful Practices: A New Generation of Workers Has Discovered Encouraging Alternatives." *Mission Frontiers*, July-August 2008: 6-10.

Allen, Don, Rebecca Harrison, Eric Adams, Laura Adams, Bob Fish, and E. J. Martin. "Fruitful Practices: A Descriptive List." *International Journal of Frontier Missiology* 26, no. 3 (2009): 111-122.

Burke, Lawrence. A Narrative Review: Seven Fruitful Practices for Muslim Ministry. Available from *info@fruitfulpractice.org*, unpublished, 2008.

Collison, Chris, and Geoff Parcell. *Learning to Fly: Practical Knowledge Management from Leading and Learning Organizations*. Chicester, West Sussex: Capstone, 2004.

Dale, Lauren. Literature Review: Team Building in Multi-Cultural Ministries. Available from *info@fruitfulpractice.org*, unpublished, 2008.

Woodberry, J. Dudley, ed. From *Seed to Fruit: Global Trends, Fruitful Practices, and Emerging Issues among Muslims*. Pasadena, CA: William Carey Library, 2008.

www.ingramcontent.com/pod-product-compliance
Lightning Source LLC
Chambersburg PA
CBHW071342080526
44587CB00017B/2933